AINS 21 Course Guide

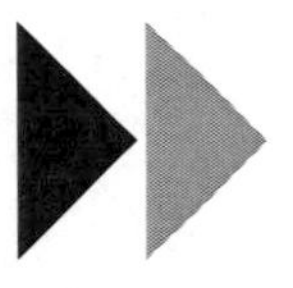

Property and Liability Insurance Principles
7th Edition

The Institutes
720 Providence Road, Suite 100
Malvern, Pennsylvania 19355-3433

Unless otherwise apparent, examples used in The Institutes materials related to this course are based on hypothetical situations and are for educational purposes only. The characters, persons, products, services, and organizations described in these examples are fictional. Any similarity or resemblance to any other character, person, product, services, or organization is merely coincidental. The Institutes are not responsible for such coincidental or accidental resemblances.

This material may contain internet website links external to The Institutes. The Institutes neither approve nor endorse any information, products, or services to which any external websites refer. Nor do The Institutes control these websites' content or the procedures for website content development.

The Institutes specifically disclaim any implied warranties of merchantability or fitness for a particular purpose. No warranty may be created or extended by sales representatives or written sales materials.

The Institutes materials related to this course are provided with the understanding that The Institutes are not engaged in rendering legal, accounting, or other professional service. Nor are The Institutes explicitly or implicitly stating that any of the processes, procedures, or policies described in the materials are the only appropriate ones to use. The advice and strategies contained herein may not be suitable for every situation.

7th Edition • 2nd Printing • December 2018

ISBN: 978-0-89462-276-2

Contents

Study Materials Available for AINS 21

Property and Liability Insurance Principles, 7th ed., 2018, AICPCU.

AINS 21 *Course Guide*, 7th ed., 2018, AICPCU (includes access code for SMART Online Practice Exams).

AINS 21 SMART Study Aids—Review Notes and Flash Cards, 7th ed.

Student Resources

Catalog A complete listing of our offerings can be found in The Institutes' professional development catalog, including information about:

- Current programs and courses
- Current textbooks, course guides, SMART Study Aids, and online offerings
- Program completion requirements
- Exam registration

To obtain a copy of the catalog, visit our website at TheInstitutes.org or contact Customer Success at (800) 644-2101.

How to Prepare for Institutes Exams This free handbook is designed to help you by:

- Giving you ideas on how to use textbooks and course guides as effective learning tools
- Providing steps for answering exam questions effectively
- Recommending exam-day strategies

The handbook is printable from the Student Services Center on The Institutes' website at TheInstitutes.org or available by calling Customer Success at (800) 644-2101.

Educational Counseling Services To ensure that you take courses matching both your needs and your skills, you can obtain free counseling from The Institutes by:

- Emailing your questions to Advising@TheInstitutes.org
- Calling an Institutes counselor directly at (610) 644-2100, ext. 7601
- Obtaining and completing a self-inventory form, available on our website at TheInstitutes.org or by contacting Customer Success at (800) 644-2101

Exam Registration Information As you proceed with your studies, be sure to arrange for your exam.

- Visit our website at TheInstitutes.org/forms to access and print the Registration Booklet, which contains information and forms needed to register for your exam.
- Plan to register with The Institutes well in advance of your exam.

How to Contact The Institutes For more information on any of these publications and services:

- Visit our website at TheInstitutes.org
- Call us at (800) 644-2101 or (610) 644-2100 outside the U.S.
- Email us at CustomerSuccess@TheInstitutes.org
- Fax us at (610) 640-9576
- Write to us at The Institutes, Customer Success, 720 Providence Road, Suite 100, Malvern, PA 19355-3433

Using This Course Guide

This course guide will help you learn the course content and prepare for the exam.

Each assignment in this course guide typically includes the following components:

Educational Objectives These are the most important study tools in the course guide. Because all of the questions on the exam are based on the Educational Objectives, the best way to study for the exam is to focus on these objectives.

Each Educational Objective typically begins with one of the following action words, which indicate the level of understanding required for the exam:

Analyze—Determine the nature and the relationship of the parts.

Apply—Put to use for a practical purpose.

Associate—Bring together into relationship.

Calculate—Determine numeric values by mathematical process.

Classify—Arrange or organize according to class or category.

Compare—Show similarities and differences.

Contrast—Show only differences.

Define—Give a clear, concise meaning.

Describe—Represent or give an account.

Determine—Settle or decide.

Evaluate—Determine the value or merit.

Explain—Relate the importance or application.

Identify or list—Name or make a list.

Illustrate—Give an example.

Justify—Show to be right or reasonable.

Paraphrase—Restate in your own words.

Recommend—Suggest or endorse something to be used.

Summarize—Concisely state the main points.

Outline The outline lists the topics in the assignment. Read the outline before the required reading to become familiar with the assignment content and the relationships of topics.

Key Words and Phrases These words and phrases are fundamental to understanding the assignment and have a common meaning for those working in insurance. After completing the required reading, test your understanding of the assignment's Key Words and Phrases by writing their definitions.

Review Questions The review questions test your understanding of what you have read. Review the Educational Objectives and required reading, then answer the questions to the best of your ability. When you are finished, check the answers at the end of the assignment to evaluate your comprehension.

Application Questions These questions continue to test your knowledge of the required reading by applying what you've studied to "hypothetical" real-life situations. Again, check the suggested answers at the end of the assignment to review your progress.

Sample Exam Your course guide includes a sample exam (located at the back) or a code for accessing SMART Online Practice Exams (which appears on the inside of the cover). Use the option available for the course you're taking to become familiar with the test format. SMART Online Practice Exams are as close as you can get to experiencing an actual exam before taking one.

More Study Aids

The Institutes also produce supplemental study tools, called SMART Study Aids, for many of our courses. When SMART Study Aids are available for a course, they are listed on page iii of the course guide. SMART Study Aids include Review Notes and Flash Cards and are excellent tools to help you learn and retain the information in each assignment.

Assignment 1
Understanding Insurance

Assignment 2
Insurance Regulation

Assignment 3
Insurer Financial Performance

Direct Your Learning

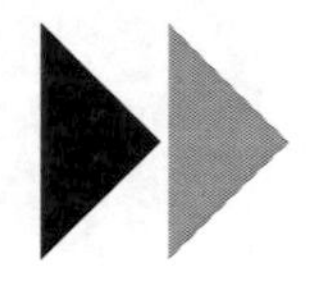

1

Understanding Insurance

Educational Objectives

After learning the content of this assignment, you should be able to:

1. Describe the benefits and the costs of insurance to individuals, organizations, and society.
2. Explain how insurance operates in different roles.
3. Distinguish among the common types of personal and commercial insurance.
4. Describe the various types of private insurers providing property and liability insurance.
5. Describe United States federal and state government insurance programs.
6. Distinguish among the following insurance functions:
   - Marketing
   - Underwriting
   - Claims
   - Risk control
   - Premium audit

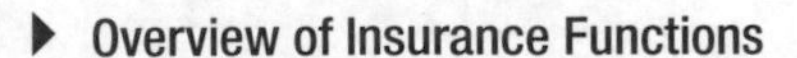

Outline

- Benefits and Costs of Insurance
  - A. The Benefits of Insurance
    1. Managing Cash Flow Uncertainty
    2. Meeting Legal Requirements
    3. Promoting Risk Control
    4. Enabling Efficient Use of Resources
    5. Providing Support for Insureds' Credit
    6. Providing a Source of Investment Funds
    7. Reducing Social Burdens
  - B. The Costs of Insurance
- Major Roles of Insurance
  - A. Insurance as a Risk Management Technique
  - B. Insurance as a Risk Transfer System
  - C. Insurance as a Business
  - D. Insurance as a Contract
- Common Types of Personal and Commercial Insurance
  - A. Personal Insurance
    1. Property and Liability Insurance
    2. Life and Health Insurance
  - B. Commercial Insurance
- Types of Private Insurers
  - A. Stock Insurers
  - B. Mutual Insurers
  - C. Reciprocal Insurance Exchanges
  - D. Lloyd's
  - E. Surplus Lines Insurers
  - F. Captive Insurers
  - G. Reinsurance Companies
- Government Insurance Programs
  - A. Reasons for Government Insurance Programs
    1. Fill Unmet Needs in the Private Insurance Market
    2. Facilitate Compulsory Insurance Purchases
    3. Provide Efficiency in the Market and Convenience to Insureds
    4. Achieve Collateral Social Purposes
  - B. Level of Government Involvement
  - C. Common Examples of Federal and State Programs
- Overview of Insurance Functions
  - A. Marketing
  - B. Underwriting
  - C. Claims
  - D. Risk Control
  - E. Premium Audit

When reviewing for your exam, remember to allot time for frequent breaks.

For each assignment, you should define or describe each of the Key Words and Phrases and answer each of the Review and Application Questions.

Educational Objective 1

Describe the benefits and the costs of insurance to individuals, organizations, and society.

Key Word or Phrase

Internet of Things (IoT)

network of objects that transmit data to and from w/out human interaction.

Review Questions

1-1. Identify the benefit that is often considered the main purpose of insurance.

Helping insureds regain footing after a loss.

1-2. Explain how insurance can provide insureds with the incentive to undertake risk control measures.

risk-sharing mechanisms - deductibles, premium credit, contracts.

1-3. Explain how insurance can provide a source of investment funds.

bonds, stock market. premium collection to pay claims. promote economic growth.

▶▶

1-4. Identify the four main costs of insurance.

- premiums paid by insureds
- operating costs of insurers
- opportunity costs
- increased losses.

Educational Objective 2

Explain how insurance operates in different roles.

Key Words and Phrases

Big data

sets of data that are too big to be gathered & analyzed by traditional methods.

Law of large numbers

math principle - # of independent exposures increase, the future losses also increase.

Property-casualty insurance

1 of 2. main sectors, types of insurance, homeowners, auto, commercial.

Utmost good faith

obligation to act in complete honesty and disclose relevant facts

Contract of adhesion

any contract in take it or leave it, must accept or reject the contract.

Contract of indemnity

contract which insurer agrees to pay amount directly related to amount of the loss.

▶▶

Review Questions

2-1. Identify the four major roles in which insurance operates.

- risk management technique
- risk transfer system
- Business
- Contract

2-2. Explain how the decision-making process used to determine which risk management technique best suits an insured's needs has evolved.

More reliant on technology & big data

2-3. Describe how insurance works as a risk transfer system.

premiums paid, insurers cover losses.

predict the number of losses

2-4. Identify the primary sources of income for an insurer.

premiums, income produced

2-5. Explain how an insurance policy is also a contract of indemnity.

Insurance may not pay for loss in full, but what is paid is related to loss & insured will not profit.

Educational Objective 3

Distinguish among the common types of personal and commercial insurance.

Key Words and Phrases

Homeowners policy

covers prop & liability.
protects insureds home & contents by causes of loss.

Personal auto policy (PAP)

Covers individual policy that covers individual arising out of ownership, maintenance & use of auto

Commercial general liability (CGL) insurance

Common liability faced by an organization including operations, premises & products.

Workers compensation insurance

provides cov. for benefits an employer is obligated to pay under workers comp laws.

Review Questions

3-1. Describe the property coverage provided by a homeowners policy.

home and contents

fire wind & lightning

3-2. Describe two typical personal liability loss exposures and how a personal umbrella liability policy could provide needed protection

Cost to repair or replace. Juries often award large sums of money. and assests to protect. high limits of personal liability ?

3-3. Distinguish between the two main categories of life insurance.

Term life - lasts for a period of time, does not accrue cash value

permament life - life time protection, accrues cash value

3-4. Identify the fundamental purpose of an annuity.

perodic income that individual cannot outlive

3-5. Identify the purpose of commercial package policies and businessowners policies.

property, crime & liability coverages

3-6. Identify four common causes of loss covered by auto physical damage coverage.

Collision, fire, theft, Collision w/ animal

▶▶

3-7. Identify the purpose of environmental liability insurance.

business owners protection against
environmental damage.
remediation & clean up. leaking fuel tank.

3-8. Describe the coverage provided by workers compensation insurance.

pays cost of medical care lost wages
& other state-mandated benefits
when employees are injured on job or
illness.

Educational Objective 4

Describe the various types of private insurers providing property and liability insurance.

Key Words and Phrases

Stock insurer

owned by stockholders formed as a
corporation to earn a profit.

Mutual insurer

owned by policy holders formed as a
corporation for purpose of providing insurance.

Lloyd's (Lloyd's of London)

association of investors, grouped in syndicates
represented by underwriters to write insurance &
reinsurance.

Surplus lines insurer

non admitted insurer eligible to insure risks that have
been exported by surplus line w/ surplus lines law.

Nonadmitted insurer

insurer not authorized by state insurance
to do business within that state

▶▶

Captive insurer

Formed primarily to cover loss exposures of its parent or members

Reinsurance

Transfer of risk from one insurer to another through contractual agreement.

Review Questions

4-1. Explain one of the primary objectives of a stock insurer.

returning profit to its stockholders

4-2. Describe the role of a stock insurer's board of directors.

authority to appoint a CEO & control insurance activities

4-3. Explain two similarities between mutual insurers and stock insurers regarding earnings.

profit & dividends.

▶▶

4-4. Identify five activities an attorney-in-fact of a reciprocal insurance exchange undertakes for the subscribers.

4-5. Identify three reasons why captive insurers are an important insurance-buying alternative for corporations.

Application Question

4-6. Allen runs a business that is getting ready to start manufacturing a new product, but the production process is tricky and introduces new risks. Because of the potential for large losses, standard market insurers will not accept an application from Allen for coverage at this time. Explain the kind of insurer that might provide Allen with coverage.

Educational Objective 5

Describe United States federal and state government insurance programs.

Review Questions

5-1. Identify four main purposes of government insurance programs.

5-2. Explain why government programs are needed to facilitate compulsory insurance purchases.

5-3. Describe how government insurance programs improve market efficiency.

5-4. Identify the three levels at which the government can participate in an insurance program.

5-5. Provide common examples of federal government insurance programs.

5-6. Provide common examples of state government insurance programs.

Educational Objective 6

Distinguish among the following insurance functions:

- **Marketing**
- **Underwriting**
- **Claims**
- **Risk control**
- **Premium audit**

Key Words and Phrases

Underwriting

Business process management (BPM)

Risk control

Premium audit

Review Questions

6-1. Identify the five functions insurers perform to balance the goal of protecting their customers with the goal of earning a profit.

6-2. Explain the role of the underwriting function.

6-3. Identify the six activities that are included in the claims handling process.

6-4. Describe how the risk control function can support underwriters in selecting which losses to insure.

6-5. Explain why the premium audit function may be necessary at the end of a policy period.

Answers to Assignment 1 Questions

NOTE: These answers are provided to give students a basic understanding of acceptable types of responses. They often are not the only valid answers and are not intended to provide an exhaustive response to the questions.

Educational Objective 1

1-1. The best-known benefit of insurance, which is often considered its main purpose, is helping insureds regain their footing after a loss. Provided that the loss is to a covered loss exposure and involves a covered cause of loss, an insurer will indemnify the insured, subject to any applicable deductibles and policy limits.

1-2. Insurance can provide insureds with the incentive to undertake cost-effective risk control measures through risk-sharing mechanisms, such as deductibles, premium credit incentives, and contractual requirements, as well as through collected data that can be used to prevent or limit losses before they happen.

1-3. Having a robust insurance plan can help an insured financially because the funds that an insured would otherwise have to retain in order to pay for large potential losses can instead be invested in bonds, the stock market, or development projects. Similarly, insurers can invest the funds that they collect in premiums until they are needed to pay insureds' claims.

1-4. These are the four main costs of insurance :

- Premiums paid by insureds
- Operating costs of insurers
- Opportunity costs
- Increased losses

Educational Objective 2

2-1. Insurance operates in each of these four major roles:

- As a risk management technique
- As a risk transfer system
- As a business
- As a contract

2-2. The decision-making process used to determine which risk management technique best suits an insured's needs has become more reliant on technology and big data. Insurance professionals can use an abundance of new data to analyze an insured's history and needs. They can then recommend coverages, as well as risk control and loss prevention techniques that could make the recommended coverages more affordable.

2-3. Insurance enables a person, a family, or an organization to transfer the costs of losses to an insurer. The insurer, in turn, pays claims for covered losses from the premiums it has collected and, in effect, distributes the costs of the losses among all its insureds.

2-4. The primary sources of revenue for insurers are premiums and the income produced from investing premiums between the time they are collected and the time they are used to pay covered claims.

2-5. An insurance policy does not necessarily pay the full amount necessary to restore an insured who has suffered a covered loss to the same financial position, but the amount the insurer pays is directly related to the amount of the insured's loss and will not enable the insured to profit from the loss.

Educational Objective 3

3-1. The property coverage provided by a homeowners policy protects insureds for damage to the home and its contents caused by fire, wind, lightning, and other causes of loss.

3-2. Two typical personal liability loss exposures and how a personal umbrella liability policy could provide needed protection are those in which a jury awards a large sum of money in a liability case and when a homeowner has significant assets to protect and therefore requires higher limits of insurance than those available under personal liability or personal auto coverage.

3-3. There are two main categories of life insurance: term life insurance and permanent life insurance. Term life insurance provides coverage for a specified period, such as ten or twenty years, with no cash value and may be an effective risk management strategy for young families who cannot afford high premiums but need protection for a parent's premature death. Permanent life insurance provides coverage until death, and, in contrast with term life insurance, its premiums remain consistent throughout the life of the policy.

3-4. The fundamental purpose of an annuity is to provide periodic income that an individual cannot outlive.

3-5. The purpose of commercial package policies and businessowers policies is to provide business owners with the necessary property, crime, and liability coverages in one policy.

3-6. Four common causes of loss covered by auto physical damage coverage are collision, fire, theft, and collision with an animal.

3-7. The purpose of environmental liability insurance is to protect business owners against environmental damage that may occur as a result of business operations.

3-8. Workers compensation insurance pays the cost of medical care, lost wages, and other state-mandated benefits when employees are injured on the job or acquire a job-related illness, such as asbestosis.

Educational Objective 4

4-1. One of the primary objectives of a stock insurer is returning a profit to its stockholders.

4-2. A stock insurer's board of directors has the authority to appoint a chief executive officer (CEO) and control the insurer's activities.

4-3. These are two examples of the similarities between mutual insurers and stock insurers regarding earnings:

- Mutual insurers generally seek to earn profits in their ongoing operations, as do stock insurers.
- A stock insurer may choose to share profits with its stockholders. Mutual insurers also may opt to share profits, but pay dividends instead to policyholders as a return of a portion of premiums paid.

4-4. In a reciprocal insurance exchange, an attorney-in-fact acts on behalf of the subscribers to market and underwrite insurance coverage, collect premiums, invest funds, and handle claims.

4-5. These are three reasons why captive insurers are an important insurance-buying alternative for corporations:

- They help eliminate problems that some corporations face when necessary or desired insurance coverage is unavailable or costs more than the corporation is willing or able to pay.
- They might provide insurance coverage at a lower cost than other private insurers.
- They can provide improved cash flow because a premium paid to a captive remains within the corporate structure until it is used to pay claims.

4-6. Allen might be able to obtain coverage through a surplus lines insurer. Surplus lines insurance consists of insurance coverages unavailable in the standard market (usually because of pricing difficulties or an inability to meet underwriting requirements). As new insurance needs arise, the surplus lines market responds. Producers and consumers often turn to the surplus lines market when they have an immediate need for a new type of coverage. Surplus lines insurers can often respond quickly to these developing needs, while standard market insurers may take longer to analyze the need for new or revised coverage, and to file policy forms and rates for state approval.

Educational Objective 5

5-1. Government insurance programs exist to fill unmet needs in the private insurance market, to facilitate compulsory insurance purchases, to provide efficiency in the market and convenience to insureds, and to achieve collateral social purposes.

5-2. Government programs are needed to facilitate compulsory insurance purchases because not everyone required to purchase such insurance can obtain coverage at a reasonable price in the private market.

5-3. Government insurance programs improve market efficiency by reducing either the time or the resources insureds need to expend to obtain the desired insurance coverage.

5-4. The government can participate in an insurance program as an exclusive insurer, as a partner with a private insurer, or as an insurer in direct competition with private insurers.

5-5. Common examples of federal government insurance plans include the National Flood Insurance Program (NFIP) and federal crop insurance.

5-6. Examples of state government insurance programs include workers compensation plans, residual auto plans, and beach and windstorm plans.

Educational Objective 6

6-1. To balance the goal of protecting their customers with the goal of earning a profit, insurers perform these five functions:

- Marketing
- Underwriting
- Claims
- Risk control
- Premium audit

6-2. The role of the underwriting function is to determine how much coverage the insurer should offer for a given loss exposure, as well as at what price and under what conditions the coverage should be offered.

6-3. When evaluating a claim, the adjuster typically applies a claims handling process that includes these six activities:

a. Acknowledging a claim and assigning it to a claims representative
b. Identifying the policy
c. Contacting the insured or the insured's representative
d. Investigating and documenting the claim
e. Determining cause of loss and loss amount
f. Concluding the claim

6-4. The risk control function supports underwriters in selecting which loss exposures to insure. Risk control representatives can use predictive analytics and other technology to obtain information beyond what the insurance application provides to underwriters; in turn, this can help improve decision making.

6-5. When commercial insurance policies are written, it is not uncommon for the premium to be calculated using a loss exposure measurement that could change during the policy period (usually one year). Therefore, the premium audit function, which occurs at the end of a policy period, determines whether any adjustments to the premium are required, based on the insured's actual loss exposures during that period.

Direct Your Learning

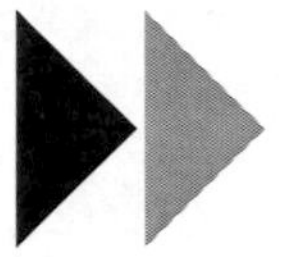

2

Insurance Regulation

Educational Objectives

After learning the content of this assignment, you should be able to:

1. Explain why insurance operations are regulated.
2. Explain how individual states in the United States regulate the licensing of insurers.
3. Summarize the regulation of insurance rates and policy forms by individual states in the United States.
4. Explain how the individual states in the United States regulate insurance marketing activities and insurer solvency.

Outline

- **Why Insurance Operations Are Regulated**
  - A. Protect Consumers
  - B. Maintain Insurer Solvency
  - C. Prevent Destructive Competition
- **Insurer Licensing**
  - A. Insurer's Licensing Status
  - B. Becoming Licensed as a Domestic Insurer
    1. Forms of Ownership
    2. Capital and Surplus
  - C. Becoming Licensed as a Foreign or an Alien Insurer
  - D. Admitted Insurers and Nonadmitted Insurers
  - E. Producers and Claims Representatives
- **Insurance Rate and Form Regulation**
  - A. Insurance Rate Regulation
  - B. Insurance Policy Form Regulation
  - C. Exemptions From Rate and Form Regulation
- **Market Conduct and Solvency Regulation**
  - A. Market Conduct
    1. Sales
    2. Underwriting
    3. Claims
  - B. Licensing
  - C. Insurer Solvency
    1. Establish Financial Requirements
    2. Conduct Field Examinations
    3. Review Annual Statements
    4. Administer IRIS

Plan to register with The Institutes well in advance of your exam. For complete information regarding exam dates and fees, please visit our website, TheInstitutes.org/forms, where you can access and print exam registration information.

For each assignment, you should define or describe each of the Key Words and Phrases and answer each of the Review and Application Questions.

Educational Objective 1

Explain why insurance operations are regulated.

Key Word or Phrase

Solvency

Review Questions

1-1. What happens when insurance rates become inadequate due to destructive competition?

1-2. Insurance policy language is usually regulated for what purpose?

1-3. Explain why insurance regulators try to maintain and enhance the financial condition of private insurers.

Educational Objective 2

Explain how individual states in the United States regulate the licensing of insurers.

Key Words and Phrases

Domestic insurer

Foreign insurer

Alien insurer

Admitted insurer

Surplus lines law

Review Questions

2-1. What are the three primary forms of an insurer's licensing status in any given state?

2-2. What are the three most common forms of insurer ownership?

2-3. Compare the organization of a stock insurer and a mutual insurer.

2-4. Describe a reciprocal insurance exchange.

2-5. Compare a foreign insurer to an alien insurer.

2-6. Describe a nonadmitted insurer, and explain how nonadmitted insurers can transact business in a state.

2-7. What is the purpose of licensing individual insurance professionals such as producers and claims representatives?

Application Question

2-8. ABC Company is an insurer incorporated and licensed in one state. ABC would like to expand into a neighboring state. What requirements will ABC need to meet in order to be licensed in the neighboring state?

Educational Objective 3

Summarize the regulation of insurance rates and policy forms by individual states in the United States.

Review Questions

3-1. Describe the three major criteria that a state insurance commissioner would consider when deciding to approve or disapprove an insurer's request for a rate.

3-2. Describe how different states meet the three major criteria for insurance rates.

3-3. Compare file-and-use rating laws with use-and-file laws.

3-4. Describe open-competition rating laws.

3-5. Identify the two major objectives of regulations regarding insurance policy forms.

3-6. Explain why surplus lines insurers are generally exempt from insurance regulations pertaining to policy forms and rates.

Application Question

3-7. A new insurer in a state that has an open-competition rating law is charging rates for auto insurance policies that are much lower than those of all of the other auto insurers in the state. Many of the other insurers express concern to the insurance commissioner that these rates are too low.

Discuss whether the insurance commissioner can take action on the complaint in an open-competition rating system. Explain your answer.

Educational Objective 4

Explain how the individual states in the United States regulate insurance marketing activities and insurer solvency.

Key Words and Phrases

Market conduct regulation

Unfair trade practices law

Reserve

Solvency surveillance

National Association of Insurance Commissioners (NAIC)

NAIC Annual Statement

Insurance Regulatory Information System (IRIS)

Guaranty fund

Review Questions

4-1. Identify the focus of market conduct regulation.

4-2. Explain what penalties can be imposed under most state unfair trade practices laws in each of these circumstances.

a. An insurance agent engages in unfair trade practices.

b. An insurer is guilty of unfair underwriting practices.

4-3. List the four methods regulators use to verify insurers' solvency.

Application Question

4-4. A state insurance department has received several complaints alleging that Insurance Company is slow to resolve claims and then denies them without explanation.

a. Explain how the department of insurance is likely to follow up on these complaints.

b. Identify the type of regulatory oversight under which insurance company operations fall.

Answers to Assignment 2 Questions

NOTE: These answers are provided to give students a basic understanding of acceptable types of responses. They often are not the only valid answers and are not intended to provide an exhaustive response to the questions.

Educational Objective 1

1-1. When insurance rate levels become inadequate, some insurers may not collect enough money to pay all of their insureds' claims and may become insolvent. Other insurers might lose so much profit that they withdraw from the market or stop writing new business. An insurance shortage can then develop, and individuals and organizations might be unable to obtain the coverage they need.

1-2. Regulators review insurance language to protect consumers. Many insurance policies are complex legal documents that may be difficult for some consumers to analyze and understand. Regulators can set coverage standards, specify policy language for certain insurance coverages, and disapprove unacceptable policies.

1-3. Insurance regulators try to maintain and enhance the financial condition of private insurers for several reasons:

- Premiums are paid in advance, and the period of protection extends into the future. If an insurer becomes insolvent, future claims might not be paid even though the premium has been paid. Consumers may find it difficult to evaluate insurers' financial ability to keep their promises.
- Regulation is needed to protect the public interest. Large numbers of individuals are adversely affected when insurers become insolvent. For example, an unusually large catastrophe that affects a large area can make an insurer's financial ability to pay claims uncertain, such as when Hurricane Andrew struck Florida in 1992 and caused seven insurer insolvencies.
- Insurers hold substantial funds for the ultimate benefit of policyholders. Government regulation is necessary to safeguard such funds.

Educational Objective 2

2-1. An insurer's licensing status in any given state may assume that of a domestic insurer, a foreign insurer, or an alien insurer.

2-2. The three most common forms of insurer ownership are stock insurance companies, mutual insurance companies, and reciprocal insurance exchanges.

2-3. Stockholders supply the capital needed to form a stock insurer or to expand its operations. Stockholders expect to receive a return on their investment in the form of stock dividends, increased stock value, or both. A mutual insurer is owned by its policyholders. Because a traditional mutual insurer issues no common stock, it has no stockholders. Stockholders and policyholders have similar voting rights and elect the insurer's board of directors.

2-4. A reciprocal insurance exchange consists of a series of private contracts in which subscribers, or members of the group, agree to insure each other.

2-5. A foreign insurer is a United States insurer that is licensed to do business in a state but is incorporated in a different state. An alien insurer is a non-U.S. insurer that is licensed to do business in the U.S. states where it wishes to operate.

2-6. A nonadmitted insurer, often referred to as a surplus lines insurer, is not authorized by the state insurance department to do business within that state. Under surplus lines laws, a nonadmitted insurer may be permitted to transact business only through a specially licensed surplus lines producer.

2-7. The examinations required for licensing, along with continuing education requirements, attempt to ensure that insurance professionals have a minimum level of insurance knowledge and meet ethical standards.

2-8. ABC will first need to show the regulator in the neighboring state that it has satisfied the requirements in its home state. ABC will also need to satisfy the minimum capital, surplus, and other requirements imposed on domestic insurers within the neighboring state.

Educational Objective 3

3-1. A state insurance commissioner would consider whether the rate is adequate; it should be sufficient to pay all claims and the expenses related to those claims, helping to maintain insurer solvency. The commissioner would also determine whether the rate is excessive and would disapprove an excessive rate; insurers are entitled to a fair return, but not to excessive or unreasonable profit. A state insurance commissioner would also consider whether the rate is unfairly discriminatory; insurers are permitted to adjust premium rates based on the risk profile of different groups of insureds, but these rates must be fair and consistent.

3-2. Different states meet these criteria by different types of rating laws that vary in the type and extent of control the states assert over insurers' rates.

3-3. Under file-and-use-laws, insurers must file rates with the state insurance department prior to their use, but the rates can be used immediately without specific approval. Use-and-file laws are a variation of the file-and-use law in which insurers file rates within a specified period of time after the rates are put into use.

3-4. In open-competition rating, market prices driven by the economic laws of supply and demand, rather than regulatory decisions, determine insurance rates. However, state insurance departments typically have the authority to monitor competition and disapprove rates if deemed necessary. The major criteria that rates must be adequate, not excessive, and not unfairly discriminatory continue to apply.

3-5. The first objective is that insurance policies be clear and readable to insurance consumers. The second major objective is to detect and address any policy provisions that are unfair or unreasonable.

3-6. Surplus lines insurers are willing to provide coverage for risks that admitted insurers are unable or unwilling to offer. Because these insurers increase the availability of insurance, they have the freedom to use policy provisions and rates that are appropriate for a particular risk.

3-7. One of the three major criteria that states consider in evaluating insurance rates is whether they are adequate. Under open-competition rating laws, the insurance commissioner has the responsibility to be sure that rates are adequate, not excessive, and not unfairly discriminatory. Therefore, the insurance commissioner can investigate the rates charged by the new insurer and take action if deemed necessary.

Educational Objective 4

4-1. Market conduct regulation focuses on how insurers treat applicants for insurance, insureds, and others who present claims for coverage.

4-2. These penalties can be imposed under most state unfair trade practices laws:

a. State regulators can suspend or revoke the licenses of sales agents or brokers who engage in unfair trade practices.

b. An insurer that is guilty of unfair underwriting practices could be fined, or its operating license could be suspended or revoked.

4-3. Regulators use these four methods to verify the solvency of insurers:

- Establish financial requirements by which to measure solvency
- Conduct on-site field examinations to ensure regulatory compliance
- Review annual financial statements
- Administer the Insurance Regulatory Information System (IRIS)

4-4. These answers relate to the state insurance department's response to complaints against Insurance Company.

a. The insurance department may investigate the complaints and may hold formal hearings as part of the investigation process. If the investigation indicates that the allegations are true, the claims representative or insurer may face a reprimand, fine, license suspension, substantial legal judgment, or another legal penalty.

b. Insurance company operations fall under market conduct regulation.

Direct Your Learning

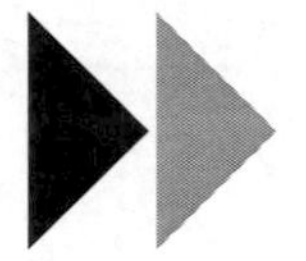

3

Insurer Financial Performance

Educational Objectives

After learning the content of this assignment, you should be able to:

1. Explain how the management of a property-casualty insurer's income and expenses determines its profitability.
2. Summarize the information found on the balance sheet and the income statement of a property-casualty insurer.
3. Analyze a property-casualty insurer's profitability information using these financial ratio calculations:
    - Loss ratio
    - Expense ratio
    - Combined ratio
    - Investment income ratio
    - Overall operating ratio
4. Given a case regarding a property-casualty insurer's financial ratio calculation(s), determine the significance of those calculation(s) on the insurer's overall financial performance.

Outline

- **Insurer Profitability and Income and Expense Management**
  - A. Managing Insurer Income
    - 1. Underwriting Income
    - 2. Investment Income
  - B. Managing Insurer Expenses
    - 1. Underwriting Activity Expenses
    - 2. Investment Activity Expenses
  - C. Insurer Profitability
- **Understanding Insurer Financial Statements**
  - A. Balance Sheet
    - 1. Assets
    - 2. Liabilities
    - 3. Policyholders' Surplus
  - B. Income Statement
- **Analyzing Insurer Financial Ratio Calculations**
  - A. Loss Ratio
  - B. Expense Ratio
  - C. Combined Ratio
  - D. Investment Income Ratio
  - E. Overall Operating Ratio
- **Knowledge to Action: Financial Ratios and Insurer Financial Performance Case**
  - A. Overview of the Procedure
  - B. Examine the Loss Ratio
  - C. Examine the Expense Ratio
  - D. Analyze the Combined Ratio

Find complete information regarding exam dates and fees at TheInstitutes.org/forms. Plan to register with The Institutes well in advance of your exam. If you have any questions, or need updated registration information, contact The Institutes.

For each assignment, you should define or describe each of the Key Words and Phrases and answer each of the Review and Application Questions.

Educational Objective 1

Explain how the management of a property-casualty insurer's income and expenses determines its profitability.

Key Words and Phrases

Loss adjustment expense (LAE)

Paid losses

Incurred losses

Incurred but not reported (IBNR) losses

Dividends

Review Questions

1-1. Identify and describe the two primary sources of an insurer's income.

1-2. Describe the components of each of these types of insurer expenses: (1) underwriting activity expenses and (2) investment activity expenses.

1-3. What financial components determine an insurer's net income before taxes?

Application Question

1-4. The Information Technology (IT) Department for QualitIn Insurance Company was concerned to learn that QualitIn had an underwriting loss for the third year in a row. What might the IT Department do to help improve QualitIn's underwriting profitability? Identify the component(s) of income or expenses that would be affected by the IT Department's action(s).

Educational Objective 2

Summarize the information found on the balance sheet and the income statement of a property-casualty insurer.

Key Words and Phrases

Assets

Admitted assets

Nonadmitted assets

Liabilities

Loss reserve

Unearned premium reserve

Policyholders' surplus

Review Questions

2-1. The balance sheet shows an insurer's financial position at a particular point in time and includes what three financial components?

2-2. Explain why an unearned premium reserve is an insurer's liability.

2-3. The income statement compares an insurer's revenue generated with the expenses incurred to produce that revenue and includes which financial components?

Application Question

2-4. Before placing a new customer's commercial property insurance with Hallidy Insurance, a company with which he was less familiar, Jerry asked his assistant to retrieve a current balance sheet for Hallidy. The assistant returned with a balance sheet dated four years prior to the current date. Explain why Jerry should avoid basing his decision on placing coverage with Hallidy solely on a four-year-old balance sheet.

Educational Objective 3

Analyze a property-casualty insurer's profitability information using these financial ratio calculations:

- **Loss ratio**
- **Expense ratio**
- **Combined ratio**
- **Investment income ratio**
- **Overall operating ratio**

Key Words and Phrases

Loss ratio

Expense ratio

Combined ratio

Investment income ratio

Review Questions

3-1. Given an insurer with a loss ratio greater than its preestablished target ratio, what is an example of an analysis it might make in finding ways to reduce its total incurred losses?

3-2. An insurer wants to take action to better meet its target expense ratio. Identify one action an insurer might take to improve each of these components of the expense ratio.

a. Written premium

b. Acquisition costs

c. General expenses

3-3. The insurance industry as a whole experiences difficulty in one year because of excessive expenses related to catastrophe losses and a poor economic environment.

a. How might that affect the average combined ratio for the industry?

b. In that same difficult year, two insurers had combined ratios that were less than 100. What would this indicate about those two insurers?

Application Question

3-4. Tamarado Insurance Company, a commercial property, liability, and workers compensation insurer, ended the past year with a combined ratio of 107 percent and an overall operating ratio of 88 percent. Answer the following questions about Tamarado's profitability.

a. What do these ratios indicate about Tamarado's profitability for that year?

b. Suggest two actions that Tamarado might take to improve its profitability for the coming year.

Educational Objective 4

Given a case regarding a property-casualty insurer's financial ratio calculation(s), determine the significance of those calculation(s) on the insurer's overall financial performance.

Application Questions

4-1. Juniquote Insurance set a goal to improve its loss ratio by 15 percent over the next year. Analyze the following proposals and determine whether each would be likely to improve Juniquote's loss ratio.

a. Juniquote will offer loss control services for its commercial insureds that exceed the services offered by its competitors.

b. Juniquote will discontinue writing homeowners insurance in two states that have the highest licensing fees (of those states where they write homeowners) and strict requirements for wording that must be used in homeowners policy provisions and all policy-related communications.

4-2. Sauguine Insurance hired an experienced investment manager to select profitable investments and to balance its investment portfolio and still meet regulatory requirements for its use of policyholders' surplus.

How might Sauguine's hire of this investment manager improve its overall gain or loss from operations?

4-3. Overlan Insurance writes a high volume of personal auto insurance throughout the United States. Because Overlan specializes in auto insurance, it offers a lower premium than any other auto insurer. Overlan is reviewing its loss ratio, expense ratio, and combined ratio to find ways to improve its combined ratio of 106 percent. The combined ratio was calculated using these figures:

Combined ratio = loss ratio + expense ratio

106% = 68% + 38%

Evaluate whether each of these proposals, in absence of other proposals, could significantly improve Overlan's combined ratio, and explain your answer.

a. Overlan will offer a 10 percent rate decrease for all of its new and existing policyholders.

b. Overlan will implement a new cost-effective system that enables prospective insureds to submit an online application for insurance. The system evaluates the risk and provides a quote to the insured in two minutes or less. The system also enables insureds to accept the quote, renew their policy online, make online premium payments, and submit most policy changes to Overlan online.

Answers to Assignment 3 Questions

NOTE: These answers are provided to give students a basic understanding of acceptable types of responses. They often are not the only valid answers and are not intended to provide an exhaustive response to the questions.

Educational Objective 1

1-1. An insurer's income is primarily composed of underwriting income and investment income. Underwriting income is generated by the sale of insurance and is the amount remaining (either a gain or a loss) after underwriting losses and expenses are subtracted from earned premiums. Investment income is generated from the insurer's investment of funds and is the amount remaining (either a gain or a loss) after investment expenses are subtracted from the gross amount earned on investments during a period.

1-2. These answers describe the components of two types of insurance expenses.

- Underwriting activity expenses include the insurer's paid and incurred losses, loss adjustment expenses, and other underwriting expenses, including acquisition expenses, general expenses (expenses associated with staffing and maintaining functional departments), and premium taxes, licenses, and fees.
- Investment activity expenses include staff salaries of professional investment managers and all other expenses related to the investment department's activities.

1-3. An insurer's net income before taxes is the sum of its total earned premiums and investment income minus its total losses and other expenses in the corresponding period, with any applicable adjustments.

1-4. Because the IT Department is not involved in underwriting, which directly affects premiums, or in claims, which directly affect losses and loss expenses, the best way for the IT Department to help improve QualitIn's underwriting profitability is to look for ways to cut expenses within its own department or to suggest ways to cut expenses for the entire organization. These expenses are general expenses of the insurer, which are a component of "other underwriting expenses." Any actions that reduce expenses will help lead to greater profitability.

Educational Objective 2

2-1. The balance sheet includes the insurer's assets, liabilities, and policyholders' surplus.

2-2. The unearned premium reserve is a liability because it represents insurance premiums prepaid by insureds for services that the insurer has not yet rendered. If the insurer ceased operations and canceled all of its policies, the unearned premium reserve would represent the total of premium refunds that the insurer would owe its current policyholders.

2-3. The income statement includes the insurer's revenue (earned premiums), expenses (incurred losses, loss adjustment expenses, and other underwriting expenses), net underwriting gain or loss, net investment income, and net income before income taxes.

2-4. An insurer's balance sheet shows its assets and liabilities only as of a particular date, a snapshot of the insurer's financial position at that point in time. The figures change constantly. Insurers establish unearned premium reserves for premiums they receive. The unearned premium reserve for each policy declines with the passage of time. Also, losses occur, and insurers establish loss reserves. New policies are written, and old policies expire or are renewed. Meanwhile, the insurer buys and sells stocks, bonds, and other investments as needed to meet its obligations while earning investment income. Because of these factors, Hallidy's balance sheet has probably changed considerably in a four-year period. Therefore, Jerry should locate a more recent balance sheet to help with his placement decision, and he may also want an income statement for the corresponding period(s).

Educational Objective 3

3-1. This is one acceptable answer:

To reduce its loss ratio, an insurer could review the types of insurance that it writes and evaluate the loss potential for those types of insurance or the territories where it writes that insurance. It could identify types of insurance or territories that are highly susceptible to losses and consider the effect of reducing the volume of such business, while increasing the volume of business it writes that is less susceptible to losses.

3-2. These are actions an insurer might take to reduce components of the expense ratio: (Answers will vary.)

a. The insurer may be able to increase its written premium while managing its growth by staying the course with a plan developed previously to support its growth mode.

b. To reduce acquisition costs, the insurer might discontinue a costly and unprofitable agency incentive program.

c. To reduce general expenses, the insurer might offer an employee incentive program to encourage employees to work more efficiently and make fewer errors.

3-3. These answers address questions regarding the insurance industry in a poor economic environment:

a. The average combined ratio for the industry for that year could be a loss (greater than 100).

b. This would indicate that those two insurers had a gain in a very difficult year. Those two insurers would stand out as exceptional insurers in a difficult insurance market.

3-4. These answers address questions regarding the Tamarado case:

a. The combined ratio of 107 percent indicates that Tamarado suffered an underwriting loss of 7 percent for that year. For every $1.00 of premium that Tamarado earned, it paid $1.07 for losses and expenses. Tamarado's overall operating ratio of 88 percent indicates that Tamarado's investments for that year were successful and that, in spite of its underwriting loss, Tamarado earned a profit on its investments and, consequently, earned an overall profit for the year.

b. Tamarado should increase its earned premiums or decrease its expenses to improve its underwriting ratio for the coming year. These actions could help improve its profitability:

- Tamarado could offer an innovative, new service for its commercial insureds and increase its premiums.

- Tamarado could reduce its legal expenses by selecting legal defense counsel that have fees and limitations that conform to the claim department's guidelines.

Educational Objective 4

4-1. These are possible answers for each of the proposals:

a. Assuming insureds take advantage of these services and the result is fewer losses or less severe losses, this proposal would decrease Juniquote's losses and, consequently, its loss adjustment expenses, leading to improvement in its loss ratio.

b. This proposal is not likely to improve Juniquote's loss ratio. Discontinuing writing homeowners insurance in these states may decrease Juniquote's operating expenses because of added processing costs and the need to maintain unique policy forms and communication forms for those two states. However, operating expenses are not a component in an insurer's loss ratio, which probably would not be affected by this proposal.

4-2. Assuming this investment manager increases Sauguine's net investment income by improving its investment earnings and reducing its investment expenses, Sauguine's improved net investment income would be added to its net underwriting gain or loss to improve its overall gain or loss from operations.

4-3. These are possible answers for each of the proposals:

a. In the absence of other proposals, this proposal could generate additional business, which may improve the expense ratio; however, Overlan's current loss ratio of 68 percent is not a problem. Alternately, reducing its premiums in a noncompetitive market could lower its earned premiums and could increase its loss ratio and its expense ratio (premiums are a component of both), and hence its combined ratio.

b. Provided the system works as specified, this proposal could probably improve Overlan's expense ratio and hence its combined ratio. This system may enable Overlan to reduce its acquisition expenses over time by minimizing or eliminating producer commissions and incentives. The submission, renewal, premium payment, and policy change features of the system could enable Overlan to reduce customer service and accounting staff, which would reduce its general expenses.

B

Assignment 4
Marketing

Assignment 5
Underwriting and Ratemaking

Assignment 6
Claims

Direct Your Learning

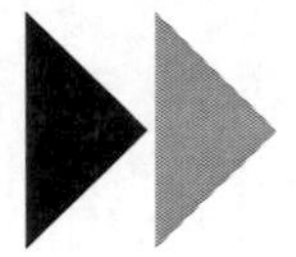

4

Marketing

Educational Objectives

After learning the content of this assignment, you should be able to:

1. Describe the factors that influence an agency relationship.
2. Summarize the various types of insurance distribution systems and alternative marketing channels.
3. Describe the functions performed by insurance producers.
4. Describe the key factors an insurer should evaluate during the distribution-system and distribution-channel selection process.

Outline

- **Understanding Factors That Influence an Agency Relationship**
  - A. Legal Roles
  - B. Legal Responsibilities
    1. Legal Responsibilities of the Agent to the Principal
    2. Legal Responsibilities of the Principal to the Agent
    3. Responsibilities to Third Parties
  - C. Scope of Authority
    1. Actual Authority
    2. Apparent Authority
- **Summarizing Types of Insurance Distribution Systems**
  - A. Independent Agency and Brokerage Marketing System
    1. Independent Agents and Brokers
    2. National and Regional Brokers
    3. Independent Agency Networks
    4. Managing General Agents
    5. Surplus Lines Brokers
  - B. Exclusive Agency Marketing System
  - C. Direct Writer Marketing System
  - D. Distribution Channels
    1. Internet
    2. Call Centers
    3. Direct Response
    4. Group Marketing
    5. Trade Associations
    6. Financial Institutions
  - E. Omnichannel Marketing System
- **Functions of Insurance Producers**
  - A. Prospecting
  - B. Risk Management Review
    1. Individual or Family
    2. Businesses
  - C. Sales
  - D. Policy Issuance
  - E. Premium Collection
  - F. Customer Service
  - G. Claim Handling
  - H. Consulting
- **Selecting Insurance Marketing Distribution Systems and Channels**
  - A. Customers' Needs and Characteristics
  - B. Insurer's Profile
    1. Insurer Strategies and Goals
    2. Insurer Strengths
    3. Existing and Target Markets
    4. Geographic Location
    5. Degree of Control Required

Plan to take one week to complete each assignment in your course.

For each assignment, you should define or describe each of the Key Words and Phrases and answer each of the Review and Application Questions.

Educational Objective 1

Describe the factors that influence an agency relationship.

Key Words and Phrases

Producer

Agent

Agency

Principal

Actual authority

Express authority

Implied authority

Binding authority

Apparent authority

Review Questions

1-1. Identify three factors that influence an agency relationship.

1-2. Identify the two essential elements of an agency relationship.

1-3. Identify the five duties that the laws of agency impose on insurance agents.

1-4. Identify three examples of the rights and duties an agency contract addresses.

1-5. Identify the legal responsibilities of the principal to the agent.

1-6. Identify the two types of actual authority.

Application Question

1-7. Alex owns and manages the Independent Insurance Agency. Alex would like to begin offering payment plans to his customers who have large insurance premiums. Alex has made arrangements with a local bank that will finance the premiums for his customers. How can Alex determine whether this type of arrangement is acceptable to the insurers that he represents?

Educational Objective 2

Summarize the various types of insurance distribution systems and alternative marketing channels.

Key Words and Phrases

Independent agency

Broker

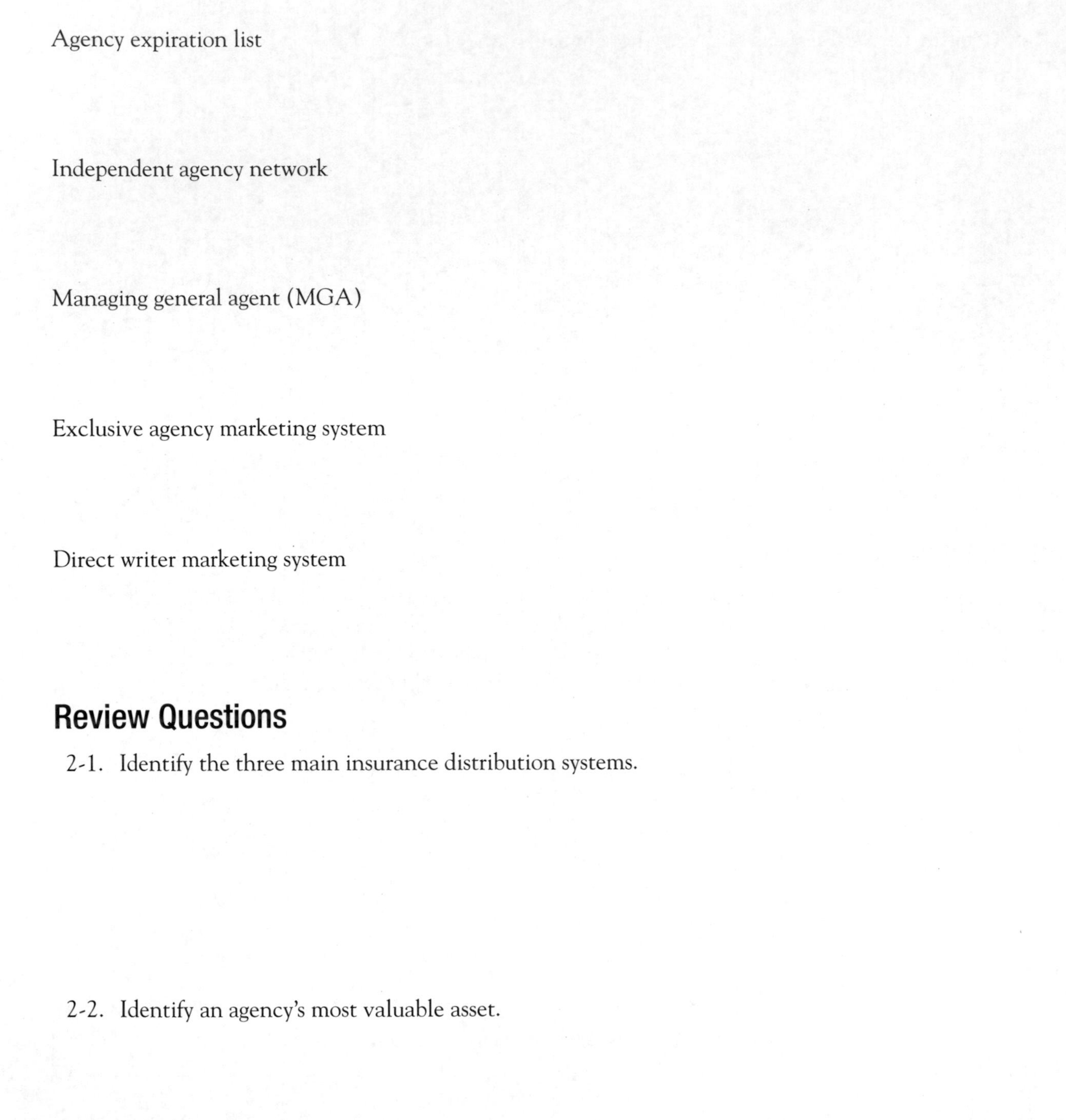

Agency expiration list

Independent agency network

Managing general agent (MGA)

Exclusive agency marketing system

Direct writer marketing system

Review Questions

2-1. Identify the three main insurance distribution systems.

2-2. Identify an agency's most valuable asset.

2-3. Identify the two typical forms of compensation for independent agents and brokers.

2-4. Identify three examples of administrative functions an exclusive agency insurer handles for the exclusive agent.

2-5. Identify two ways in which direct writer insurers can encourage their sales agents to develop new business.

2-6. Explain how insurance portals benefit customers.

2-7. Identify one advantage and one disadvantage of the direct response distribution channel.

2-8. Describe the group marketing technique of affinity marketing.

2-9. Identify the purpose of trade association advertising.

2-10. Identify the qualities of financial institutions that make them beneficial strategic partners for insurers.

2-11. Identify four issues that must be considered when using an omnichannel marketing system.

Educational Objective 3

Describe the functions performed by insurance producers.

Key Word or Phrase

Cold canvass

Review Questions

3-1. Name six methods producers use to locate prospective clients.

3-2. Describe the types of information included in a loss run that may be of use to a producer.

3-3. Identify two advantages of using qualified producers to handle claims.

Educational Objective 4

Describe the key factors an insurer should evaluate during the distribution-system and distribution-channel selection process.

Review Questions

4-1. Name the factors an insurer must evaluate relating to its profile when selecting distribution systems and channels.

4-2. Describe how assessing its internal strengths and weaknesses can help an insurer select distribution systems and channels.

4-3. Describe the considerations relating to existing markets that an insurer might evaluate when changing distribution systems and channels.

Answers to Assignment 4 Questions

NOTE: These answers are provided to give students a basic understanding of acceptable types of responses. They often are not the only valid answers and are not intended to provide an exhaustive response to the questions.

Educational Objective 1

1-1. Three factors that influence an agency relationship are legal roles, legal responsibilities, and scope of authority.

1-2. The two essential elements of an agency relationship are the agent's authority to act for the principal and the principal's control over the agent's actions on the principal's behalf.

1-3. The five duties that the laws of agency impose on insurance agents are these:

- Be loyal to the principal.
- Obey the principal's lawful instructions.
- Exercise a reasonable degree of care in actions on behalf of the principal.
- Account promptly for any of the principal's money that the agent holds.
- Keep the principal informed of all facts relating to the agency relationship. This is the duty of relaying information.

1-4. Examples of the rights and duties that an agency contract addresses include the insurance agent's right to make insurance coverage effective and any limitations on that right. The contract also specifies how the agent is to handle funds, including stipulations on how and when the agent must remit premiums to the insurer. Insurance agency contracts usually give the agent the right to employ subagents, who may act on behalf of the insurer according to the terms of the agency contract.

1-5. The legal responsibilities of the principal to the agent include these:

- Pay the agent for services performed.
- Indemnify, or reimburse, the agent for any losses or damages suffered without the agent's fault, but arising out of the agent's actions on behalf of the principal. If a third party sues the agent in connection with activities performed on behalf of the principal, the principal must reimburse the agent for any liability incurred if the agent was not at fault.

1-6. Actual authority can be express authority or implied authority.

1-7. Alex can determine whether this type of arrangement is acceptable by consulting the agency contract or agency agreement. It specifies the scope of the agent's authority and relationship with the insurer.

Educational Objective 2

2-1. The three main insurance distribution systems are the independent agency and brokerage marketing system, the exclusive agency marketing system, and the direct writer marketing system.

2-2. An agency's most valuable asset is the ownership of its expiration lists.

2-3. Compensation for independent agents and brokers may be a flat percentage commission on all new and renewal business submitted or a contingent or profit-sharing commission based on volume or loss ratio goals.

2-4. The exclusive agency insurer handles many administrative functions for the exclusive agent, including policy issuance, premium collection, and claims processing.

2-5. Direct writer insurers can encourage their sales agents to develop new business by relieving producers of nonselling activities and compensating at a lower renewal rate.

2-6. Insurance portals benefit customers by offering the products and services of many insurance providers on one website. Although the leads that portals generate must subsequently be screened and fully underwritten by the insurers accepting the coverage, they can increase an insurer's market share and brand awareness.

2-7. An advantage of direct response is that commission costs, if any, are greatly reduced. However, a disadvantage is that advertising costs are typically higher.

2-8. Affinity marketing entails insurers targeting various customer groups based on profession, interests, hobbies, or attitudes.

2-9. Trade association advertising programs are intended to create a favorable image of association members as a group and to make the public familiar with the logos and other association symbols.

2-10. Insurers view financial institutions as beneficial strategic partners because they have a strong customer base, a predisposition to product cross-selling, and strength at processing transactions. Financial institutions also efficiently use technology for database mining geared to specific products and services.

2-11. An omnichannel marketing system requires consideration of these issues: maintaining consistent customer communications, providing a consistent customer experience, matching the type of insurance with an appropriate distribution system and channel, and targeting customers with relevant data.

Educational Objective 3

3-1. Prospective clients can be located using several methods:

- Referrals from present clients
- Referrals from strategic partners, such as financial institutions and real estate brokers
- Advertising in multimedia and direct mail
- Interactive websites, social media, and mobile marketing
- Telephone solicitations
- Cold canvass

3-2. Loss runs include, at a minimum, lists of losses and their total cost. For large commercial customers, the producer may work with the customer's Risk Management Department in identifying loss exposures and risk analysis. Based on this analysis, risk treatment decisions, including insurance coverage, can be made. The producer can then coordinate further coverage discussions between the customer and the insurer.

3-3. Claims handling by qualified producers offers two major advantages: quicker service to policyholders and lower loss adjustment expenses to the insurer.

Educational Objective 4

4-1. An insurer must evaluate these factors relating to its profile when selecting distribution systems and channels:

- Its strategies and goals
- Its strengths
- Its existing and target markets
- Its geographic location
- Its desired or needed degree of control over producers

4-2. Once an insurer determines where its strengths lie, it selects those distribution systems and channels that maximize its opportunities to capture market share and minimize its weaknesses.

4-3. The characteristics of an insurer's existing book of business should be considered before any change in distribution system or channel. If agents or brokers own the expirations for current accounts, the insurer must either give up that business and start over or purchase the expirations from producers. Either option might be expensive, depending on the quality of the existing business. The insurer should also consider the possibility that a change in distribution systems and channels could disrupt communication channels, which may result in policyholder dissatisfaction and lost accounts.

Direct Your Learning

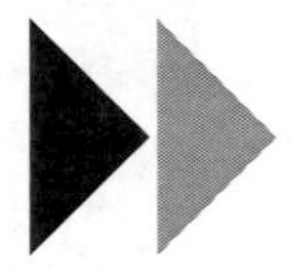

5

Underwriting and Ratemaking

Educational Objectives

After learning the content of this assignment, you should be able to:

1. Distinguish among the underwriting activities typically performed by line and staff underwriters.
2. Describe the steps in the underwriting process.
3. Summarize the responsibilities of underwriting management.
4. Explain how insurance rates are developed.
5. Given the insurance rate and exposure units for a particular insurance policy, calculate the policy premium.

Outline

- **Underwriting Activities**
  - A. Line Underwriting Activities
  - B. Staff Underwriting Activities
- **The Underwriting Process**
  - A. Evaluate the Submission
    - 1. Weigh the Need for Information
    - 2. Gather the Necessary Information
  - B. Develop Underwriting Alternatives
  - C. Select an Underwriting Alternative
  - D. Determine an Appropriate Premium
  - E. Implement the Underwriting Decision
  - F. Monitor the Underwriting Decision
    - 1. Monitor Individual Policies
    - 2. Monitor Books of Business
- **Underwriting Management**
  - A. Participating in Insurer Management
  - B. Arranging Reinsurance
  - C. Delegating Underwriting Authority
  - D. Developing and Enforcing Underwriting Guidelines
  - E. Monitoring Underwriting Results
- **Ratemaking**
  - A. Insurance Advisory Organizations
  - B. Insurance Rating Systems
    - 1. Loss Costs
    - 2. Class Rating
    - 3. Individual Rating
    - 4. Final Rate and Premium Determination
- **Premium Determination**
  - A. Insurance Rates
  - B. Exposure Units
  - C. Calculation of Premium (Rate x Exposure Units)
  - D. Other Factors Affecting Premium Determination

Studying before sleeping helps you retain material better than studying before undertaking other tasks.

For each assignment, you should define or describe each of the Key Words and Phrases and answer each of the Review and Application Questions.

Educational Objective 1

Distinguish among the underwriting activities typically performed by line and staff underwriters.

Key Words and Phrases

Line underwriter

Staff underwriter

Adverse selection

Underwriting guidelines (underwriting guide)

Policyholders' surplus

Underwriting policy (underwriting philosophy)

Prospective loss costs

Loss development

Trending

Underwriting authority

Underwriting audit

Review Questions

1-1. Describe line underwriting activities.

1-2. Describe the line underwriter responsibility of account classification.

1-3. Describe how a line underwriter may respond to questions from producers and applicants about how coverage will respond to a particular type of loss.

1-4. Identify examples of goals for a book of business that a line underwriter works to help achieve.

1-5. Explain why line underwriters have a vested interest in ensuring that producers' and insureds' needs are met.

1-6. Identify how staff underwriters can monitor line underwriters' activities and their adherence to underwriting authority.

Educational Objective 2

Describe the steps in the underwriting process.

Key Words and Phrases

Underwriter

Loss exposure

Hazard

Information efficiency

Loss run

Predictive analytics

Predictive modeling

Catastrophe model

Experience rating

Schedule rating

Retrospective rating plan

Certificate of insurance

Review Questions

2-1. List all six steps in the underwriting process.

2-2. List five principal sources of underwriting information.

2-3. Describe the four major ways an underwriter can modify a submission.

2-4. Describe factors other than the content of a submission that an underwriter must consider before selecting an underwriting alternative.

2-5. Describe what insurance loss costs are typically based on.

2-6. Identify examples of events that trigger the monitoring of existing policies.

Educational Objective 3

Summarize the responsibilities of underwriting management.

Key Words and Phrases

Treaty reinsurance

Facultative reinsurance

Review Questions

3-1. Identify the responsibilities underwriting management entails.

3-2. Provide examples of the kinds of decisions made at an insurer's senior-management level.

3-3. What is the distinction between treaty reinsurance and facultative reinsurance?

3-4. Identify the primary factors that influence the authority given to an underwriter.

3-5. Identify the elements listed in underwriting guidelines.

3-6. What is the purpose of constant monitoring of underwriting results?

Educational Objective 4

Explain how insurance rates are developed.

Key Words and Phrases

Ratemaking

Actuary

Machine learning

Loss costs

Insurance advisory organization

Contingencies

Class rating

Individual rate, or specific rate

Judgment rating

Final rate

Review Questions

4-1. Describe the role of insurance advisory organizations in ratemaking.

4-2. Explain why insurers often adjust data on historical loss costs in the ratemaking process.

4-3. What is the basic premise of an insurance classification and rating system?

Application Question

4-4. Interstate Trucking Company (ITC) has sixty employees. Among them are forty truck drivers who spend 95 percent of their time on the road. The organization also has seven customer service representatives who handle telephone calls and schedule shipments from the home office. Under ITC's workers compensation insurance, which group of employees would the company pay more to insure? Explain.

Educational Objective 5

Given the insurance rate and exposure units for a particular insurance policy, calculate the policy premium.

Key Words and Phrases

Rate

Rate manual

Exposure unit (unit of exposure)

Review Questions

5-1. Describe how underwriters use the Insurance Services Office, Inc. (ISO) *Commercial Lines Manual* (CLM) to determine premiums.

5-2. Describe the use of exposure units in insurance rating.

5-3. Provide two examples of exposure units.

5-4. Explain how to calculate a commercial insurance premium using the rate and exposure unit.

5-5. Why might an underwriter vary from the manual rate when determining premium?

5-6. What is the purpose of schedule rating plans?

Application Questions

5-7. A movie theater is applying for commercial general liability insurance. The rate is $100 per 1,000 admissions. The insurer estimates that the theater will have 50,000 admissions in the new policy period. Calculate the premium.

5-8. XYZ Company is applying for building insurance. The rate is $0.50 per $100 of building insurance. XYZ would like to insure the building for $500,000. Calculate the premium that XYZ would pay.

Answers to Assignment 5 Questions

NOTE: These answers are provided to give students a basic understanding of acceptable types of responses. They often are not the only valid answers and are not intended to provide an exhaustive response to the questions.

Educational Objective 1

1-1. Line underwriting activities include selecting insureds, classifying and pricing accounts, recommending or providing coverage, management a book of business, supporting producers and customers, and coordinating with marketing.

1-2. Line underwriters are responsible for account classification, which is the process of grouping accounts with similar attributes so that they can be priced appropriately.

1-3. Line underwriters may respond to questions from producers and applicants about how coverage will respond to a particular type of loss by explaining the types of losses covered and the endorsements that can be added to provide coverage not included in standard policies.

1-4. The line underwriter works to ensure that each book of business achieves established goals, such as product mix, loss ratio, and written premium.

1-5. Line underwriters have a vested interest in ensuring that producers' and insureds' needs are met because customer service activities and underwriting are often interwoven.

1-6. Staff underwriters are often responsible for monitoring line underwriters' activities and their adherence to underwriting authority, which can be evaluated by conducting underwriting audits.

Educational Objective 2

2-1. The underwriting process entails these six steps:

- Evaluate the submission
- Develop underwriting alternatives
- Select an underwriting alternative
- Determine an appropriate premium
- Implement the underwriting decision
- Monitor the underwriting decision

2-2. Principal sources of underwriting information include producers, applications, inspection reports, government records, financial rating services, loss data, and claims files.

2-3. An underwriter can modify a submission in these four ways:

- Require implementation of additional risk control measures
- Change insurance rates, rating plans, or policy limits
- Amend policy terms and conditions
- Use facultative reinsurance

2-4. The underwriter must consider these additional factors before selecting an underwriting alternative:

- Underwriting authority
- Supporting business
- Mix of business
- Producer-underwriter relationships
- Regulatory restrictions

2-5. Insurance loss costs are typically based on an elaborate classification system in which similar loss exposures are combined into the same rating classification.

2-6. Existing policies are usually monitored in response to any of these triggering events:

- Substantive policy changes
- Significant and unique losses
- Preparation for renewal
- Risk control and safety inspections
- Premium audits

Educational Objective 3

3-1. The responsibilities of an insurer's underwriting management include these:

- Participating in the insurer's overall management
- Arranging reinsurance
- Delegating underwriting authority
- Developing and enforcing underwriting guidelines
- Monitoring underwriting results

3-2. Decisions made at an insurer's senior-management level might determine what type of marketing system the insurer uses, office locations, the emphasis that will be placed on personal and commercial insurance, and so forth.

3-3. The distinction between treaty reinsurance and facultative reinsurance is that treaty reinsurance automatically reinsures all eligible policies, while facultative reinsurance involves a separate transaction for each reinsured policy.

3-4. The authority given to an underwriter usually reflects the underwriter's experience and responsibilities and the types of insurance handled.

3-5. Underwriting guidelines list the factors that should be considered by the underwriter for each type of insurance, the desirable and undesirable characteristics of applicants relative to those factors, and the insurer's overall attitude toward applicants that exhibit those characteristics.

3-6. Constant monitoring of underwriting results enables underwriting management to adjust underwriting guidelines to accommodate changing conditions, goals, and results.

Educational Objective 4

4-1. Insurance advisory organizations help develop insurance rating systems by collecting reliable loss data that insurers use in establishing their rates and premiums. The organizations analyze the loss data collected to determine the average loss costs per exposure unit used in class rating.

4-2. Insurers often adjust data on historical loss costs in anticipation of losses that can be expected in the future as a result of inflation or other measurable trends. The resulting prospective loss costs indicate the amount of money an insurer can expect to pay for future claims for each exposure unit.

4-3. The basic premise of an insurance classification and rating system is that insureds with similar characteristics have similar potential loss frequency and severity. Even though wide variation in actual losses may occur from one insured to the next, aggregate losses among all members of the class should be predictably different from the losses of all members of another class who have different characteristics.

4-4. ITC would pay more for workers compensation insurance covering its truck drivers for several reasons. First, the drivers represent a higher number of loss exposure units. Second, long hours spent driving expose truck drivers to more traffic accidents than customer service representatives. And third, as a class, truck drivers suffer more frequent and more severe injuries and disabilities. The rating class for truck drivers reflects this significantly higher loss exposure; the employer pays a higher rate for the higher loss exposure.

Educational Objective 5

5-1. The ISO *CLM* provides classification tables that contain hundreds of classifications of commercial business operations. When calculating the premium for commercial accounts, underwriters typically determine the insured's business operation and then find the appropriate rating classification in the applicable classification table.

5-2. The fundamental measures of the loss exposures used in insurance rating are referred to as exposure units. Insurers use standardized exposure units for rating most types of insurance.

5-3. Examples of exposure units include these:

- Auto—each vehicle
- Commercial property—each $100 of insured value
- General liability—each $1,000 of gross sales (for example, a restaurant or retail store); each 1,000 of square feet of area (for example, a school); each $1,000 of payroll (for example, a consulting firm); each 1,000 admissions (for example, a movie theater)
- Homeowners—each $1,000 of insured value
- Workers compensation—each $100 of payroll

5-4. The number of exposure units is multiplied by the insurance rate.

5-5. Underwriters vary from the manual rate to reflect the reality of actual exposures to loss, the specific characteristics of those exposures, and competitive market influences.

5-6. Underwriters use schedule rating plans to reflect the differences between the applicant and the average risk. Underwriters apply scheduled rating credits to "better-than-average" risks and scheduled debits to "worse-than-average" risks.

5-7. The premium for the movie theater can be calculated in this way:

Admissions ÷ unit size = Number of exposure units

50,000 admissions ÷ 1,000 admissions = 50 exposure units

Rate per unit x Number of exposure units = Premium

$100 x 50 = $5,000

5-8. The premium that XYZ Company would pay can be calculated in this way:

Insured value ÷ Unit size = Number of exposure units

$500,000 ÷ $100 = 5,000 units

Rate per unit x Number of exposure units = Premium

$0.50 x 5,000 = $2,500

Direct Your Learning

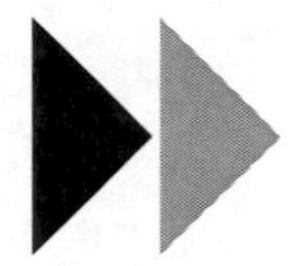

6

Claims

Educational Objectives

After learning the content of this assignment, you should be able to:

1. Illustrate how an insurer's claims function supports these primary goals:
   - Keeping the insurer's promise
   - Supporting the insurer's profit goal
2. Examine how Claims Department results can be optimized by:
   - Department structure
   - The types and functions of claims personnel
   - Claims performance measurements
3. Describe the activities in the claims handling process.
4. Explain how claims representatives handle these aspects of property insurance claims:
   - Verifying coverage
   - Determining the amount of loss
   - Concluding the claim
5. Explain how claims representatives handle these aspects of liability insurance claims:
   - Verifying coverage
   - Determining the cause of loss
   - Determining the amount of damages
   - Concluding the claim
6. Examine the elements of good-faith claims handling.

Outline

- **Goals of the Claims Function**
  - A. Keeping the Insurer's Promise
  - B. Supporting the Insurer's Profit Goal
- **Claims Department Structure, Personnel, and Performance**
  - A. Claims Department Structure
  - B. Claims Personnel
    - 1. Staff Claims Representatives
    - 2. Independent Adjusters
    - 3. Third-Party Administrators
    - 4. Producers
    - 5. Public Adjusters
  - C. Claims Performance Measures
    - 1. Profitability Measures
    - 2. Quality Measures
- **The Claims Handling Process**
  - A. Acknowledging and Assigning the Claim
  - B. Identifying the Policy
  - C. Contacting the Insured or the Insured's Representative
  - D. Investigating the Claim
  - E. Documenting the Claim
  - F. Determining the Cause of Loss, Liability, and the Loss Amount
  - G. Concluding the Claim
    - 1. Payments
    - 2. Claim Denial
    - 3. Alternative Dispute Resolution and Litigation
    - 4. Closing Reports
- **Aspects of Property Insurance Claims**
  - A. Verifying Coverage
  - B. Determining the Amount of Loss
    - 1. Common Valuation Methods
    - 2. Valuation Process
  - C. Concluding the Claim
  - D. Special Considerations for Property Catastrophe Claims
- **Aspects of Liability Insurance Claims**
  - A. How Liability Claims Differ From Property Claims
  - B. Verifying Coverage
  - C. Determining the Cause of Loss
  - D. Determining the Amount of Damages
    - 1. Compensatory Damages
    - 2. Punitive Damages
  - E. Concluding the Claim
- **Good-Faith Claims Handling**
  - A. Law of Bad Faith
  - B. Elements of Good-Faith Claims Handling
    - 1. Thorough, Timely, and Unbiased Investigation
    - 2. Complete and Accurate Documentation
    - 3. Fair Evaluation
    - 4. Good-Faith Negotiation
    - 5. Regular and Prompt Communication
    - 6. Competent Legal Advice
    - 7. Effective Claims Management

Repetition helps students learn. Read, write, and repeat key points for each assignment.

For each assignment, you should define or describe each of the Key Words and Phrases and answer each of the Review and Application Questions.

Educational Objective 1

Illustrate how an insurer's claims function supports these primary goals:

- **Keeping the insurer's promise**
- **Supporting the insurer's profit goal**

Key Words and Phrases

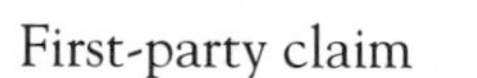

First-party claim

Third-party claim

Claimant

Claims representative

Review Questions

1-1. Name two primary goals of the claims function.

1-2. Explain the contractual promise an insurer agrees to fulfill and how it fulfills this promise.

1-3. Describe how these claims function personnel help the insurer generate an underwriting profit.

a. Claims managers

b. Claims staff

c. Claims representatives

Application Question

1-4. Jason, a claims manager for Insurance Company, held a meeting of the claims representatives in his department. Jason asked the claims representatives to identify specific ways that they can help the company comply with its contractual promise and support its profit goals. From the viewpoint of a claims representative in this meeting, explain the claims representatives' roles in fulfilling these two goals of the claims function.

Educational Objective 2

Examine how Claims Department results can be optimized by:

- **Department structure**
- **The types and functions of claims personnel**
- **Claims performance measurements**

Key Words and Phrases

Third-party administrator (TPA)

Independent adjuster

Public adjuster

Review Questions

2-1. Describe these claims personnel:

a. Staff claims representatives

b. Independent adjusters

c. Third-party administrators (TPAs)

d. Producers

e. Public adjusters

2-2. Identify the two types of performance measures used to evaluate a Claims Department's performance.

Application Questions

2-3. Musgrove Insurance has received a claim related to an accident that involved an aircraft, and an investigation is needed to process the claim. The problem is, the company doesn't have any available field claims representatives with knowledge about aircraft. Identify the type of claims professional the company would hire to help with the investigation.

2-4. You are a claims representative attempting to settle a complex claim for an insured. Unfortunately, the insured is not satisfied with the way settlement negotiations are progressing. Identify whom the insured might hire to ensure that its interests are protected in the claims process.

2-5. Management is evaluating an insurer's financial well-being, and it wants to know whether the Claims Department is functioning properly, whether the Underwriting Department is selecting appropriate loss exposures, and whether the Actuarial Department is pricing the insurance products correctly. Describe the profitability measure that can make these determinations.

Educational Objective 3

Describe the activities in the claims handling process.

Key Words and Phrases

Nonwaiver agreement

Reservation of rights letter

Subrogation

Mediation

Arbitration

Appraisal

Mini-trial

Summary jury trial

Review Questions

3-1. Identify the goal of assigning a claim.

3-2. If it is apparent from the loss notice that coverage may not be available for the loss, the claims representative should prepare either one of which two documents to notify the insured of this concern while still preserving the insurer's rights?

3-3. Explain why establishing and maintaining adequate reserves is important for an insurer's financial stability.

3-4. Explain why establishing reserves for liability claims can be difficult.

3-5. When an insurer pays a claim to an insured for a loss caused by a negligent third party, how can the insurer recover that payment amount from that negligent third party?

3-6. Identify three crucial parts of claims documentation.

3-7. What do claims representatives use to determine the cause of a loss?

3-8. Identify examples of alternative dispute resolution (ADR) techniques.

▶▶

Educational Objective 4

Explain how claims representatives handle these aspects of property insurance claims:

- **Verifying coverage**
- **Determining the amount of loss**
- **Concluding the claim**

Key Words and Phrases

Insurable interest

Actual cash value (ACV)

Depreciation

Replacement cost

Agreed value method

Salvage rights

Review Questions

4-1. Identify the three crucial components of the claims handling process for property insurance claims.

4-2. What are the three steps involved in initial verification of coverage?

4-3. Identify the four questions for which the claims representative must seek answers to verify that a claim is covered.

4-4. When determining the amount of loss for a personal property claim, what is the most important information?

4-5. Identify the most common property valuation methods.

4-6. Identify the three factors that can be used to determine the replacement cost of real property.

4-7. Provide examples of factors that can complicate the negotiation phase of the property insurance claims process.

4-8. What are salvage rights?

Application Question

4-9. A covered cause of loss destroys a family's three-year-old television. The television would cost $800 to replace with a comparable (of like kind and quality) new television. A television is generally expected to be used for six years. Explain how the claims representative would determine the covered television's actual cash value (ACV).

Educational Objective 5

Explain how claims representatives handle these aspects of liability insurance claims:

- **Verifying coverage**
- **Determining the cause of loss**
- **Determining the amount of damages**
- **Concluding the claim**

Key Words and Phrases

Damages

Compensatory damages

Special damages

General damages

Punitive damages (exemplary damages)

Review Questions

5-1. Identify the four key aspects of claims handling for liability insurance claims.

5-2. Identify three reasons why liability claims adjusting differs from and may be more difficult than property claims adjusting.

5-3. Describe the process a claims representative follows to verify that a property claim is covered.

5-4. Describe damages.

5-5. Identify the purpose of compensatory damages.

5-6. Identify the purpose of punitive damages.

Educational Objective 6

Examine the elements of good-faith claims handling.

Review Questions

6-1. Explain why claims representatives' actions may be closely scrutinized and are often criticized.

6-2. Why do most bad-faith claims for breach of the implied duty of good faith and fair dealing arise under insurance-related contracts rather than other types of contracts?

6-3. Identify the elements of good-faith claims handling.

6-4. Identify the elements of a thorough claims investigation.

6-5. Explain why promptness is a crucial element of fair claim evaluation.

6-6. Identify how claims representatives should resolve disputes over settlement amounts.

6-7. Explain why communicating with all parties to a claim is a crucial aspect of good-faith claims handling and resolving claims.

Answers to Assignment 6 Questions

NOTE: These answers are provided to give students a basic understanding of acceptable types of responses. They often are not the only valid answers and are not intended to provide an exhaustive response to the questions.

Educational Objective 1

1-1. The two primary goals of the claims function are compliance with the contractual promise and support of the insurer's profit goal.

1-2. The contractual promise that the insurer fulfills, as set out in the insuring agreement, is to pay, defend, or indemnify the insured in the event of a covered loss. The insurer fulfills this promise by providing fair, prompt, and equitable service to the policyholder, either directly for first-party claims or indirectly for third-party claims.

1-3. These are ways in which the following claims function personnel help the insurer generate an underwriting profit:

a. Claims managers help the insurer generate an underwriting profit by managing all claims function expenses, setting appropriate spending policies, and using appropriately priced providers and services.

b. Claims staff can help the insurer generate an underwriting profit by avoiding overspending on costs of handling claims, claims operations, and other expenses.

c. Claims representatives help the insurer generate an underwriting profit by working to settle claims fairly, thus reducing the possibility of costly litigation and regulatory oversight or penalties.

1-4. Claims representatives help the insurer fulfill its contractual promise by handling claims in a way that promotes peace of mind for the policyholder and that quickly restores a claimant to his or her pre-loss condition. Claims representatives, along with all claims staff, can support the insurer's profit goals by avoiding overspending on claims handling, operations, and other expenses. In addition, claims representatives can help the insurer avoid costly litigation, regulatory oversight, and penalties by treating policyholders and other claimants fairly to ensure satisfaction with the claims service.

Educational Objective 2

2-1. Claims personnel can be described in these ways:

a. Staff claims representatives are employees of an insurer and handle most claims. They may include inside claims representatives, who handle claims exclusively from the insurer's office, and field claim representatives, who handle claims both inside and outside the office.

b. Independent adjusters are claims representatives with whom insurers contract to handle claims in strategic locations, to meet increased service demand, or when special skills are needed.

c. Self-insured businesses may contract with TPAs, who handle claims, keep claims records, and perform statistical analyses. TPAs are often associated with large independent adjusting firms or with subsidiaries of insurers.

d. Producers can function as claims representatives for certain claims. The term "producer" includes agents, brokers, sales representatives, and intermediaries who place insurance with insurers. Insurers may allow producers the authority to pay claims up to a certain amount. Those producers can issue claim payments, called drafts, directly to insureds for covered claims, thus reducing an insured's wait time.

e. A public adjuster is an organization or a person hired by an insured to represent the insured in a claim in exchange for a fee. In general, the public adjuster prepares an insured's claim and negotiates the settlement with the staff claims representative or independent adjuster.

2-2. The two types of performance measures used to evaluate a Claims Department's performance are profitability measures and quality measures.

2-3. Musgrove Insurance would hire an independent adjuster to help with its aircraft investigation. Insurers use independent adjusters to meet desired service levels or when specialized skills are needed, and because no field claims representatives at Musgrove have knowledge about aircraft, the company must seek assistance from an independent adjuster.

2-4. To ensure that its interests are protected in the claims process, the insured described might hire a public adjuster. A public adjuster is an outside organization or person who represents the insured in a claim. In general, the public adjuster prepares an insured's claim and negotiates the settlement with the staff claims representative or independent adjuster. The insured, in turn, pays the public adjuster's fee, which is usually a percentage of the settlement.

2-5. Management would use a loss ratio, which compares an insurer's losses and loss adjustment expenses to its collected premiums and reveals the percentage of premiums being consumed by losses.

Educational Objective 3

3-1. The goal is to assign the claim to a claims representative who possesses the appropriate skills to handle it.

3-2. The two documents that preserve the insurer's rights when coverage is doubtful are a nonwaiver agreement and a reservation of rights letter. The claims representative should prepare either one of the two documents in such a situation.

3-3. Establishing and maintaining adequate reserves is important for an insurer's financial stability because reserves affect the insurer's ability to maintain and increase business.

3-4. Establishing reserves for liability claims can be difficult because the eventual payment on a liability claim, which may not be made for several years after the claim is made, can vary significantly from the original reserve.

3-5. When an insurer pays a claim to an insured for a loss caused by a negligent third party, the insurer can recover that payment amount from the negligent third party through the right of subrogation.

3-6. Three crucial parts of the claims documentation are diary systems, file status notes, and file reports.

3-7. Claims representatives use the facts of the loss to determine the cause of the loss.

3-8. Examples of ADR techniques include mediation, arbitration, appraisals, mini-trials, and summary jury trials.

Educational Objective 4

4-1. The three crucial components of the claims handling process for property insurance claims are verifying coverage, determining the amount of loss, and concluding the claim and exercising subrogation and salvage rights.

4-2. The three steps involved in initial verification of coverage are these:

a. Confirming that a valid policy was in effect

b. Determining that the date of the loss falls within the policy period

c. Establishing whether the damaged property is insured under the policy

4-3. The four questions for which the claims representative must seek answers to verify that a claim is covered are these:

- Does the insured have an insurable interest in the property?
- Is the damaged property covered by the policy?
- Is the cause of loss covered by the policy?
- Do any additional coverages, endorsements, or coverage limitations apply?

4-4. For personal property, the most important information is what property was damaged or destroyed.

4-5. The most common property valuation methods are actual cash value, replacement cost, and agreed value.

4-6. The replacement cost of real property can be determined using these three factors:

- Square footage of the property
- Type and quality of construction
- Construction cost per square foot

4-7. Factors that can complicate the negotiation phase of the property insurance claims process include a large number of damaged items, property of high value, or disagreement between the insured and the claims representative regarding the value or circumstances of the loss.

4-8. Salvage rights are the insurer's rights to recover and sell or otherwise dispose of insured property on which the insurer has paid a total loss or a constructive total loss.

4-9. The claims representative must place a value on the television by determining the extent of depreciation that should be considered. Because a television might be used for six years and is now three years old, the claims representative estimates the depreciation from normal wear at 50 percent. Therefore, with a replacement cost of $800 and depreciation estimated at 50 percent, the ACV of the destroyed television is $400. A payment of $400 would indemnify the insured for the loss of the television.

Educational Objective 5

5-1. The four key aspects of claims handling for liability insurance claims are verifying coverage, determining the cause of loss, determining the amount of damages, and concluding the claim.

5-2. Liability claims adjusting differs from and may be more difficult than property claims adjusting for three reasons. First, the claimant is a third party who has been injured or whose property has been damaged by the insured. Second, a liability claim may involve bodily injury. Third, liability claim settlement sometimes involves a claim for damage to the property of others that the insured has allegedly caused, which adds the difficulty of determining whether the insured is legally responsible for the property damage.

5-3. The process a claims representative follows to verify that a property claim is covered includes checking whether a valid policy was in effect and, if so, determining whether the date of the loss falls within the policy period and whether any additional coverages, endorsements, or coverage limitations apply. The claims representative must also determine whether the insured is legally responsible for the loss.

5-4. Damages are money claimed by or a monetary award to a party who has suffered bodily injury or property damage for which another party is legally responsible.

5-5. Compensatory damages are intended to compensate a victim for harm actually suffered. They include special damages and general damages.

5-6. The purpose of punitive damages is to punish the wrongdoer and to deter others from committing similar acts.

Educational Objective 6

6-1. Claims representatives' actions may be closely scrutinized and are often criticized because interactions with claims representatives are often the only personal contacts that the general public has with an insurer.

6-2. Most bad-faith claims for breach of the implied duty of good faith and fair dealing arise under insurance-related contracts rather than other types of contracts because, in insurance contracts, the insurer not only dictates the terms of the contract (the policy), but also usually controls the claims investigation, evaluation, negotiation, and settlement and therefore has more "bargaining power" than the insured.

6-3. Good-faith claims handling consists of these elements:

- Thorough, timely, and unbiased investigation
- Complete and accurate documentation
- Fair evaluation
- Good-faith negotiation
- Regular and prompt communication
- Competent legal advice
- Effective claim management

6-4. For an investigation to be considered thorough, claims representatives should collect all relevant and necessary evidence, develop the information and documentation necessary to determine liability and damages, and make decisions when they believe they have sufficient information to do so. In a thorough investigation, the claims representative is alert for new information that may change the course of the claim.

6-5. Promptness is a crucial element of fair claim evaluation because compliance with statutory time limits for completion of evaluations of coverage and damages can help reduce the insurer's exposure to bad-faith claims. Promptness is also important in responding to the claimant, the insured, or their respective lawyers' demands. Promptness is particularly important when there is a demand for settlement that is at or near the policy limits.

6-6. To resolve disputes over settlement amounts, claims representatives should use policy provisions, such as arbitration clauses, when applicable.

6-7. Communicating with all parties to a claim is a crucial aspect of good-faith claims handling and resolving claims. Keeping insureds informed is especially important because they expect it, they are most likely to make a bad-faith claim, and they may have the most important information about an accident.

Assignment 7
Risk Management

Assignment 8
Loss Exposures

Assignment 9
Insurance Policies

Direct Your Learning

7

Risk Management

Educational Objectives

After learning the content of this assignment, you should be able to:

1. Describe the basic purpose and scope of risk management.
2. Explain how to identify and analyze loss exposures.
3. Appraise the various risk control and risk financing techniques.
4. Explain how to select and implement the appropriate risk management techniques, and monitor a risk management program.
5. Explain how risk management benefits businesses, individuals, families, society, and insurers.
6. Applying the risk management process, recommend appropriate risk management techniques for handling loss exposures of an individual, a family, or a business.

Outline

- **Basic Purpose and Scope of Risk Management**
  - A. Risk Management for Individuals and Organizations
  - B. Traditional Risk Management and Enterprise-Wide Risk Management
- **Identifying and Analyzing Loss Exposures**
  - A. Identifying Loss Exposures
    1. Physical Inspection
    2. Loss Exposure Surveys
    3. Loss History Analysis
  - B. Analyzing Loss Exposures
    1. Loss Frequency
    2. Loss Severity
- **Examining the Feasibility of Risk Management Techniques**
  - A. Risk Control
    1. Avoidance
    2. Loss Prevention
    3. Loss Reduction
    4. Separation
    5. Duplication
  - B. Risk Financing
    1. Retention
    2. Transfer
- **Selecting, Implementing, and Monitoring Risk Management Techniques**
  - A. Selecting the Appropriate Risk Management Techniques
    1. Selection Based on Financial Criteria
    2. Selection Based on Informal Guidelines
  - B. Implementing the Selected Risk Management Techniques
    1. Deciding What Should Be Done
    2. Deciding Who Should Be Responsible
    3. Communicating Risk Management Information
    4. Allocating Costs of the Risk Management Program
  - C. Monitoring Results and Revising the Risk Management Program

- **Benefits of Risk Management**
  - A. Benefits of Risk Management to Businesses
  - B. Benefits of Risk Management to Individuals and Families
  - C. Benefits of Risk Management to Society
  - D. Benefits of Risk Management to Insurers
- **Applying the Risk Management Process**
  - A. Tony and Maria
  - B. Identifying and Analyzing Loss Exposures
  - C. Examining, Selecting, and Implementing Risk Management Techniques
  - D. Monitoring Results and Revising the Risk Management Program

Writing notes as you read your materials will help you remember key pieces of information.

For each assignment, you should define or describe each of the Key Words and Phrases and answer each of the Review and Application Questions.

Educational Objective 1

Describe the basic purpose and scope of risk management.

Key Words and Phrases

Pure risk

Speculative risk

Risk management

Review Questions

1-1. Explain how risk management practices differ between individuals and organizations.

1-2. Describe the difference in scope between traditional risk management and enterprise-wide risk management.

1-3. Explain how the focus of risk management efforts differs for traditional risk management and enterprise-wide risk management.

Educational Objective 2

Explain how to identify and analyze loss exposures.

Review Questions

2-1. Identify three of the most commonly used tools for identifying loss exposures.

2-2. Explain what is examined in a physical inspection to identify the loss exposures for a business.

2-3. If a particular type of loss occurs frequently, or if its frequency has been increasing in recent years, describe what the risk manager may decide to do to deal with the loss exposure.

Application Question

2-4. Rachael, an entrepreneur, is beginning a risk management program for her small Internet consulting business. She rents office space and owns the computer equipment and diagnostic tools that she uses in her business. Rachael has identified her loss exposures and found that her business is subject to professional liability exposures. Because Rachael is educated and experienced in her business, her loss frequency should be minimal, but the potential loss severity from defending a significant claim could be financially crippling for Rachael's business. If bad publicity from such a claim resulted in similar actions, professional liability claims could destroy her business. Explain why Rachael should not retain her entire liability loss exposure.

Educational Objective 3

Appraise the various risk control and risk financing techniques.

Key Words and Phrases

Avoidance

Loss prevention

Loss reduction

Retention

Review Questions

3-1. In general, what is the goal of risk control techniques?

3-2. Identify the two main objectives of an inspection report.

3-3. Give an example of each of these risk financing techniques.

a. Partial retention

b. Noninsurance risk transfer

Application Question

3-4. To handle the loss exposures of the apartment buildings she owns, Mandy has purchased apartment buildings in four different cities that are spread throughout the state of Texas. She selected properties that were inland enough that they would not be affected by hurricane winds or flooding. She also purchased a property and liability insurance policy on the apartment buildings, with a $2,000 deductible on each building. Identify the risk management techniques that Mandy has used to manage her apartment loss exposures.

Educational Objective 4

Explain how to select and implement the appropriate risk management techniques, and monitor a risk management program.

Review Questions

4-1. Describe the two common methods for selecting risk management techniques.

4-2. Identify the decisions a risk manager make to effectively implement a risk management program.

4-3. Identify what is involved in monitoring and revising the risk management program.

Application Question

4-4. Raymond is the risk manager for Sansseam Industries, a million-dollar direct marketing company for ladies clothing. Raymond has identified ten risk management techniques that he believes may be valuable for Sansseam's risk management program. Explain an appropriate method for Raymond to use to assess the ten risk management techniques.

Educational Objective 5

Explain how risk management benefits businesses, individuals, families, society, and insurers.

Review Questions

5-1. Describe how a business can benefit from risk management.

5-2. Explain how individuals and families can benefit from risk management.

5-3. Describe how society as a whole benefits from risk management.

5-4. Explain how insurers benefit from risk management.

Application Question

5-5. Maria is the head of a family household. Her teenage son has just purchased his first vehicle and is questioning the value of purchasing insurance. He is complaining that it is too expensive and he can afford only minimum limits. Describe how Maria can apply the benefits of risk management to individuals and families to encourage her son to purchase adequate insurance coverage.

Educational Objective 6

Applying the risk management process, recommend appropriate risk management techniques for handling loss exposures of an individual, a family, or a business.

Application Questions

6-1. Donald is the sole proprietor of a small used auto sales business. He has no employees. In order to develop a risk management program, Donald identified and analyzed his business loss exposures and determined that he should purchase property and liability insurance. He also purchased coverage for business interruption. Donald selected a $100,000 deductible on his business property policy because he believed he could retain that amount of loss. Shortly after Donald purchased his insurance policies, the business sustained an $85,000 vandalism loss for damage to some of the inventory and the building. Donald paid for this loss, depleting most of his business savings account.

Donald has completed the first five steps in the risk management process. Explain how the vandalism loss would be considered in the last step in the risk management process.

6-2. Gayle owns a small independent insurance agency. The agency offers property and liability insurance coverages from four insurers to prospective and existing clients. Gayle rents office space from Tyler Property Management and owns her office furnishings and equipment, including three computers and two laser jet printers. Gayle's agency maintains investments totaling $1 million. Gayle pays two customer service representatives to meet with customers, complete and submit insurance applications, help handle insurance claims, and issue agency drafts. Gayle pays for continuing education for herself and her employees to enable them to maintain their agents' licenses in their state. Attending educational seminars sometimes involves business travel. Gayle has recognized the need for a risk management program.

a. Identify the first two steps of the risk management process and apply them to the information provided on Gayle's agency.

b. Evaluate each of these risk management techniques and explain how each could apply to Gayle's agency: avoidance, loss prevention or loss reduction, insurance, and retention.

6-3. Dave and Gloria have developed and implemented a risk management program for their household. They own their home and four autos. Each is the primary operator of one of the autos, and their teenage son and daughter each use one of the other vehicles. The couple owns a motor boat, and they enjoy taking their family, and sometimes friends, along when they take the boat to a nearby lake for recreation. The couple's risk management program includes property (real and personal) and liability insurance for their home, autos, and boat and a $1 million umbrella policy. They installed a security and fire alarm system for their home and pay a fee for related services. The couple also purchased life insurance policies on themselves and their children. To monitor and revise their risk management program, Dave and Gloria must consider any changes to their situation. For each event below, suggest a change to their risk management program and identify the risk management technique. Treat each event independently of the other.

a. Dave and Gloria's sixteen-year-old son, Zach, has a hobby of rock climbing. Zach started rock climbing with a group of teenagers from his school. Because of his advanced experience, Zach often led the other teens in their excursions.

b. Dave was advised that his job was being downsized. He eventually found another job, but he accepted a significant pay cut. The couple found that they could not afford to pay the insurance that they paid in the past, but they love their home and need four autos for their family.

Answers to Assignment 7 Questions

NOTE: These answers are provided to give students a basic understanding of acceptable types of responses. They often are not the only valid answers and are not intended to provide an exhaustive response to the questions.

Educational Objective 1

1-1. Individuals and families often practice risk management informally (purchasing insurance policies and contributing to savings plans) without explicitly following a risk management process. In smaller organizations, risk management is not usually a dedicated function, but one of many tasks carried out by the owner or senior manager. In many larger organizations, the risk management function is conducted as part of a formalized risk management program.

1-2. The scope of traditional risk management is on losses generated by pure, as opposed to speculative, risks.

The scope of enterprise-wide risk management encompasses all types of risk with the intent of maximizing the organization's value.

1-3. Traditional risk management focuses on managing safety, purchasing insurance, and controlling financial recovery from losses generated by hazard risk. Enterprise-wide risk management focuses on managing all of the organization's key risks and opportunities with the intent of maximizing the organization's value.

Educational Objective 2

2-1. Three of the most commonly used tools for identifying loss exposures are physical inspections of the premises, loss exposure surveys, and loss history analyses.

2-2. During a physical inspection to identify the loss exposures of a business, a risk manager should inspect all locations, operations, maintenance routines, safety practices, work processes, and other activities in which the organization is involved.

2-3. If a particular type of loss occurs frequently, or if its frequency has been increasing in recent years, the risk manager may decide that it's time to implement corrective procedures for controlling the risk.

2-4. Rachael should not retain her entire professional liability loss exposure because even though the loss frequency for this loss exposure is expected to be low, the probable loss severity is high and difficult to calculate.

Educational Objective 3

3-1. Risk control techniques attempt to decrease the frequency and/or severity of losses or make them more predictable.

3-2. These are the two main objectives of an inspection report:

- To provide a thorough description of the applicant's operation so that the underwriter can make an accurate assessment when deciding whether to accept the application for insurance

- To provide an evaluation of the applicant's current risk control measures and recommend improvements in risk control efforts

3-3. These are some possible examples of risk financing techniques:

a. When an insured purchases insurance with a deductible and an insured loss occurs, the deductible results in a partial retention (the deductible amount) of the insured's loss exposure.

b. A hold-harmless provision included in a lease that enables the landlord to transfer the financial consequences of a liability exposure arising out of the tenant's activities is a noninsurance risk transfer technique. In this case, the hold-harmless agreement might state that the tenant agrees to indemnify the landlord for any damages the landlord becomes legally obligated to pay because of injury or damage occurring on the premises occupied by the tenant.

3-4. Mandy used these techniques to manage her apartment loss exposures:

- Mandy's purchase of apartment buildings that are geographically spread is a separation technique.
- Mandy's selection of properties that are inland to avoid hurricane winds and flooding is an avoidance technique.
- Mandy's purchase of insurance on the apartment buildings is a transfer technique.
- Mandy's selection of a $2,000 deductible on each building applies a retention technique for that portion of the loss exposure.

Educational Objective 4

4-1. Organizations and households select risk management techniques based on financial criteria or informal guidelines:

- Selection based on financial criteria—By forecasting how selection of a particular risk management technique will affect profits or output, an organization can choose the risk management technique that is likely to be the most financially beneficial.
- Selection based on informal guidelines—Most households and small organizations follow informal guidelines in selecting risk management techniques. Four guidelines might be used to select techniques: not retaining more than you can afford to lose, not retaining large exposures to save a little premium, not spending a lot of money for a little protection, and not considering insurance a substitute for risk control.

4-2. The risk manager must decide what should be done, who should be responsible, how to communicate the risk management information, and how to allocate the costs of the risk management program.

4-3. To monitor and modify the risk management program, the risk manager must periodically identify and analyze new and existing loss exposures and then reexamine, select, and implement appropriate risk management techniques.

4-4. Raymond should consider Sansseam's objectives for increasing profits and/or operating efficiency. He should forecast how each of the ten techniques will affect profits or output and choose those techniques that are likely to be the most financially beneficial in meeting Sansseam's objectives.

Educational Objective 5

5-1. This is how a business can benefit from risk management :

- Improved access to affordable insurance
- Increased opportunities for the insured
- Achievement of business goals through better management of loss exposures

5-2. This is how individuals and families can benefit from risk management:

- Ability to cope more effectively with financial disasters
- Greater peace of mind because loss exposures are under control
- Reduction in expenses by handling loss exposures in the most economical fashion
- Ability to continue activities following an accident or other loss
- Incentive to take more chances and make more aggressive decisions

5-3. This is how society as a whole benefits from risk management:

- Reduction in the number of persons dependent on society for support
- Fewer disruptions in the economic and social environment
- Stimulation of economic growth

5-4. This is how insurers benefit from risk management:

- Risk management creates a positive effect on an insurer's underwriting results, loss ratio, and overall profitability.
- Risk management provides more knowledgeable consumers of insurance.
- Risk management stimulates insurers to create innovative products and maintain competitive prices and services.

5-5. These benefits could encourage Maria's son to purchase adequate insurance coverage:

- Coping with financial disasters—"If you cause an accident, the insurance will pay for the damage to the other vehicles and for the injuries to the other passengers. Otherwise, they may sue you personally and it could disrupt your standard of living."
- Enjoying greater peace of mind—"With insurance, you can be sure that your loss exposures are under control and handled cost-effectively."
- Continuing activities following an accident—"If you purchase insurance to cover your car, you will be able to repair this vehicle or buy another one if this one is damaged in an accident."

Educational Objective 6

6-1. The last step in the risk management process is monitoring results and revising the risk management program. In completing this step, Donald's vandalism loss experience indicates that Donald overlooked the need for loss prevention or reduction techniques. He may need to implement some techniques, such as installing a tall fence around his auto lot and contracting with a security company to help prevent losses. He might also consider reducing his property deductible. Donald has to restart the risk management process based on his experiences.

6-2. These are possible answers for the questions regarding Gayle's case.

a. The first two steps of the risk management process are identifying and analyzing loss exposures. To identify her loss exposures, Gayle should create an inventory of her business personal property. She should also complete a loss control survey to help identify the business's exposure to liability losses, including the liability for injury losses to her two employees. Gayle must use her property inventory and the survey to analyze the frequency and severity of risk associated with those loss exposures. For example, one or both of her employees could be killed in an auto accident if they rode together to attend an educational seminar. This risk is relatively small, but the cost of such a loss would be severe. Because Gayle's employees may need to handle cash and other deposits and may issue claim drafts, Gayle should consider the possible frequency and severity of the employee dishonesty exposure, as well.

b. These are possible answers for each of the techniques:

- Avoidance—To reduce the risk that both of her employees could be injured while traveling, Gayle might implement a procedure specifying that only one of her employees can be out of the office on business at a time or that they can never travel in the same vehicle.
- Loss prevention or loss reduction—Gayle should consider actions that could help to minimize losses in her agency, such as installing locks, a security system, and smoke detectors, and training her staff in emergency procedures. Developing procedures for handling cash, other deposits, and managing agency drafts could help reduce the risk of robbery or theft, including employee theft. Adequate screening of newly hired employees could also help reduce the risk of an employee dishonesty loss.
- Insurance—Gayle's risk analysis could demonstrate that she should obtain a business policy that provides coverage for her business furnishings and equipment and to cover her business liability related to clients and prospective clients that conduct business with the agency. Gayle should also consider the need for coverage for errors or omissions that she or her employees make when conducting business, and she should consider the need for business interruption insurance. Finally, she should consider the need for workers compensation coverage.
- Retention—Gayle might determine that it would be cost-effective to self-insure her business property and equipment risk and she might determine that her business's investments would enable her to retain the risk of employee theft as opposed to purchasing employee dishonesty coverage.

6-3. These are possible answers for Dave and Gloria's case.

a. Dave and Gloria could consider insurance transfer of the additional liability they might face because of Zach's leading other teenagers on rock climbing excursions. They might consider increasing their umbrella limit of liability.

b. Dave and Gloria might use a risk avoidance technique. They could sell the motor boat, which would enable them to eliminate the property and liability premiums they paid for the boat.

Direct Your Learning

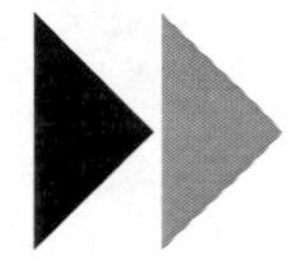

8

Loss Exposures

Educational Objectives

After learning the content of this assignment, you should be able to:

1. Describe property loss exposures in terms of assets exposed to loss, causes of loss, financial consequences of loss, and parties affected by loss.
2. Explain how legal liability to pay damages can be based on torts, contracts, or statutes.
3. Describe liability loss exposures in terms of assets exposed to loss, causes of loss, and financial consequences of loss.
4. Describe personnel loss exposures in terms of assets exposed to loss, causes of loss, and financial consequences of loss.
5. Describe net income loss exposures in terms of assets exposed to loss, causes of loss, and financial consequences of loss.
6. Describe the characteristics of an ideally insurable loss exposure.

Outline

- **Property Loss Exposures**
  - A. Assets Exposed to Property Loss
    1. Buildings
    2. Personal Property Contained in Buildings
    3. Money and Securities
    4. Vehicles and Watercraft
    5. Property in Transit
  - B. Causes of Property Loss
  - C. Financial Consequences of Property Losses
  - D. Parties Affected by Property Losses
    1. Property Owners
    2. Secured Lenders
    3. Property Holders
- **The Basis for Legal Liability**
  - A. Legal Foundations
    1. Sources of Law
    2. Criminal Law and Civil Law
    3. Damages
  - B. Torts
    1. Negligence
    2. Intentional Torts
    3. Strict Liability
  - C. Contracts
  - D. Statutes
- **Liability Loss Exposures**
  - A. Assets Exposed to Liability Loss
  - B. Causes of Liability Loss
    1. Autos, Watercraft, and Other Vehicles
    2. Premises
    3. Personal Activities
    4. Business Operations
    5. Completed Operations
    6. Products
    7. Advertising
    8. Pollution
    9. Liquor
    10. Professional Activities
  - C. Financial Consequences of Liability Loss
    1. Damages
    2. Defense Costs
    3. Damage to Reputation
- **Personnel Loss Exposures**
  - A. Assets Exposed to Personnel Loss
    1. Individual Employees
    2. Owners, Officers, and Managers
    3. Groups of Employees
  - B. Causes of Personnel Loss
    1. Death
    2. Disability
    3. Resignation, Layoffs, and Firing
    4. Retirement
    5. Kidnapping
  - C. Financial Consequences of Personnel Losses
- **Net Income Loss Exposures**
  - A. Assets Exposed to Net Income Loss
  - B. Causes of Net Income Loss
    1. Property Loss
    2. Liability Loss
    3. Personnel Loss
    4. Business Risks
  - C. Financial Consequences of Net Income Losses
- **Ideally Insurable Loss Exposures**
  - A. Pure Risk
  - B. Fortuitous Losses
  - C. Definite and Measurable
  - D. Large Number of Similar Exposure Units
  - E. Independent and Not Catastrophic
  - F. Affordable

Perform a final review before your exam, but don't cram. Give yourself between two and four hours to go over the course work.

For each assignment, you should define or describe each of the Key Words and Phrases and answer each of the Review and Application Questions.

Educational Objective 1

Describe property loss exposures in terms of assets exposed to loss, causes of loss, financial consequences of loss, and parties affected by loss.

Key Words and Phrases

Fixture

Money

Securities

Auto

Mobile equipment

Recreational vehicle

Peril

Mortgagee

Mortgagor

Bailee

Review Questions

1-1. Describe the two characteristics shared by boilers and machinery.

1-2. Explain why, for insurance purposes, money and securities are separate from other types of contents.

1-3. Explain how a reduction in value might occur if repaired property is worth less than it would have been if it had never been damaged.

1-4. What does a bailee have to consider when estimating property loss exposures?

Application Question

1-5. Josh and Jill own their home. In addition to the personal property they keep within the home, they also own two vehicles.

a. How should an insurance professional analyze Josh and Jill's property loss exposures in terms of the assets they own?

b. How should an insurance professional analyze Josh and Jill's property loss exposures in terms of causes of loss?

c. How should an insurance professional analyze Josh and Jill's property loss exposures in terms of financial consequences?

Educational Objective 2

Explain how legal liability to pay damages can be based on torts, contracts, or statutes.

Key Words and Phrases

Legal liability

Constitutional law

Statute

Statutory law

Common law (case law)

Criminal law

Civil law

Tort

Tort law

Negligence

Proximate cause

Tortfeasor

Vicarious liability

Intentional tort

Assault

Battery

Defamation

Slander

Libel

False arrest

Invasion of privacy

Strict liability (absolute liability)

Hold-harmless agreement (or indemnity agreement)

Warranty

Statutory liability

Review Questions

2-1. The legal system in the United States derives essentially from what three sources of law?

2-2. To obtain a liability judgment based on negligence, what four elements must be proven?

2-3. Describe how vicarious liability often arises in business situations.

2-4. Define strict liability (absolute liability).

2-5. Explain the reason for creating statutory liability in no-fault auto insurance laws.

Application Questions

2-6. While Gary was driving his vehicle, he approached an intersection controlled by a traffic light. His light turned green, but just as he was about to enter the intersection he noticed another vehicle coming from his left through the red light. Gary abruptly halted his vehicle, narrowly missing the oncoming vehicle. If Gary asserted a liability claim against the driver of the other car would Gary likely succeed? Explain.

2-7. Renee is a physician who provided medical care to her neighbor Susan. Tess, another neighbor, asked Renee what she treated Susan for. If Renee tells Tess, could Renee be liable for committing a tort? Explain.

Educational Objective 3

Describe liability loss exposures in terms of assets exposed to loss, causes of loss, and financial consequences of loss.

Review Questions

3-1. How does the activity of ownership, maintenance, and use of an automobile rank among the other activities in terms of the number of liability claims?

3-2. Describe how a business's publication of a person using its product could lead to a lawsuit alleging invasion of privacy.

3-3. What financial consequence will defendants and their liability insurers probably incur even if all possible lawsuits are ultimately found groundless?

Application Question

3-4. Ted operates a pet shop. A customer was examining a snake when it bit him. What activity or activities would this potential liability claim arise under?

Educational Objective 4

Describe personnel loss exposures in terms of assets exposed to loss, causes of loss, and financial consequences of loss.

Key Words and Phrases

Personnel loss exposure

Key employee

Disability

Review Questions

4-1. List several reasons why an entire group of employees may leave an organization in a short period of time.

4-2. Explain why involuntary employee separations (for example, layoffs or firings) are not considered personnel losses.

4-3. Explain why retirement is usually not as severe a loss as death or voluntary resignation.

Application Question

4-4. Abe is an insurance producer who owns his own agency as a sole proprietor. After decades of working hard to build his agency, he suffered a stroke that left him permanently and partially disabled. His doctors have told him he needs to retire immediately.

a. Describe the insurance agency's personnel loss exposures in terms of assets exposed to personnel loss.

b. Describe the insurance agency's personnel loss exposures in terms of causes of personnel loss.

c. Describe the insurance agency's personnel loss exposures in terms of financial consequences of personnel loss.

Educational Objective 5

Describe net income loss exposures in terms of assets exposed to loss, causes of loss, and financial consequences of loss.

Review Questions

5-1. Describe the asset exposed to loss in a net income loss exposure.

5-2. Contrast a direct loss with an indirect loss.

5-3. Describe a method to determine the severity of a net income loss.

Application Question

5-4. David owns and manages a fine restaurant. Describe a potential net income loss exposure of the restaurant that may result from a property loss, a liability loss, and a personnel loss.

Educational Objective 6

Describe the characteristics of an ideally insurable loss exposure.

Review Questions

6-1. Distinguish between pure risk and speculative risk.

6-2. Identify the distinguishing characteristic of a fortuitous loss.

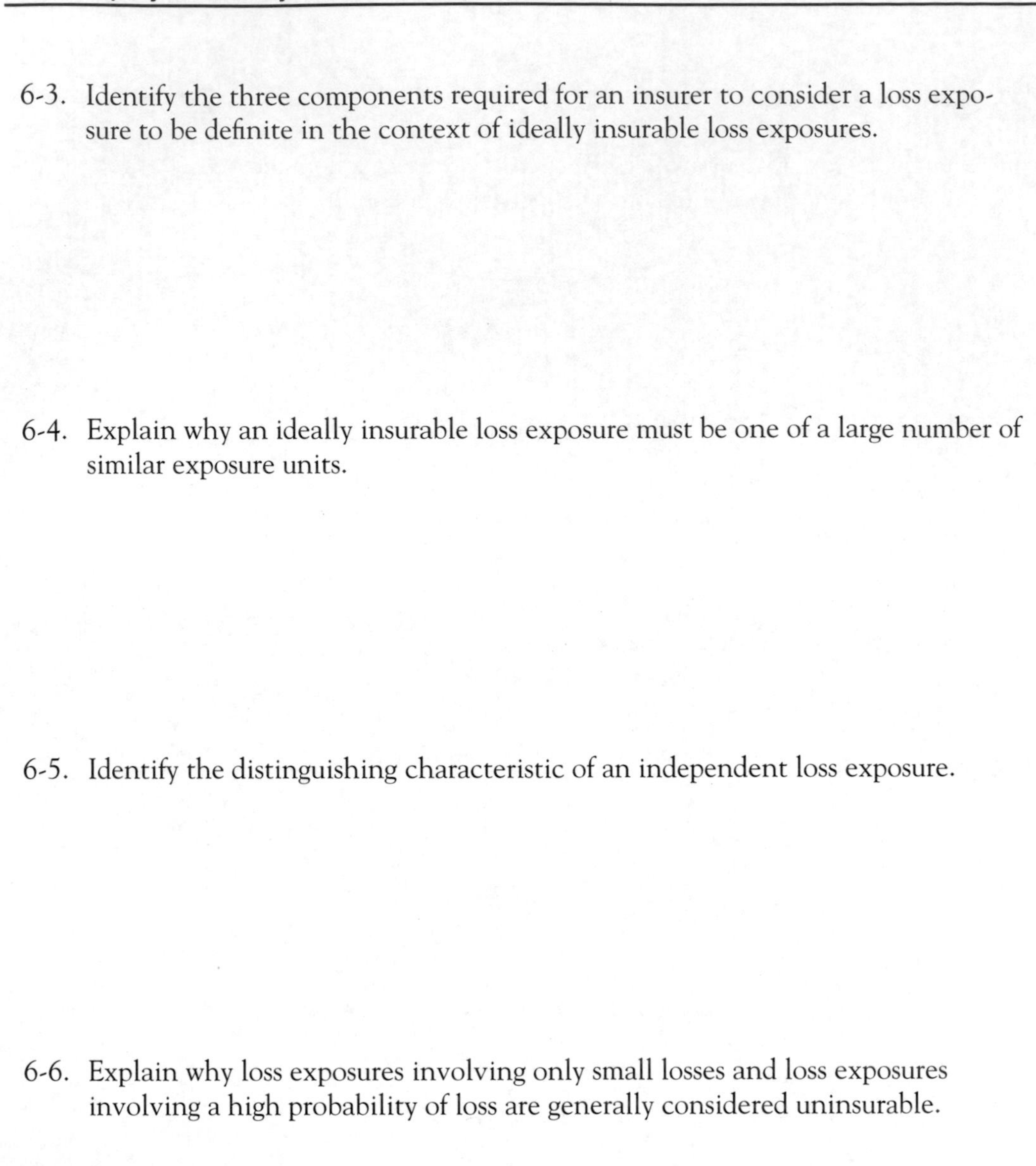

6-3. Identify the three components required for an insurer to consider a loss exposure to be definite in the context of ideally insurable loss exposures.

6-4. Explain why an ideally insurable loss exposure must be one of a large number of similar exposure units.

6-5. Identify the distinguishing characteristic of an independent loss exposure.

6-6. Explain why loss exposures involving only small losses and loss exposures involving a high probability of loss are generally considered uninsurable.

Answers to Assignment 8 Questions

NOTE: These answers are provided to give students a basic understanding of acceptable types of responses. They often are not the only valid answers and are not intended to provide an exhaustive response to the questions.

Educational Objective 1

1-1. These two characteristics are shared by boilers and machinery:

- They are susceptible to explosion or breakdown that can result in serious losses to the unit and to persons and property nearby.
- They are less likely to have explosions or breakdowns if they are periodically inspected and properly maintained.

1-2. For insurance purposes, money and securities are separate from other types of contents because their characteristics present special problems. Money and securities are highly susceptible to loss by theft. Cash is particularly difficult to trace because it can be readily spent. In contrast, other types of property must be sold for cash before the thief can make a profit. Money and securities are also lightweight, easily concealed, and easy to transport.

1-3. That a reduction in value might occur if repaired property is worth less than it would have been if it had never been damaged is true for items such as fine paintings and other art objects. Many collectibles are valuable largely because they are in mint or original condition. An object that has been repaired after damage from a tear, a scratch, or fire is no longer in that unspoiled condition, and its value will decline. The owner faces loss in the form of the cost to repair the object, as well as a reduction in value because of the altered condition.

1-4. Bailees are responsible for safekeeping property they do not own. Dry cleaners, repair shops, common carriers, and many other businesses temporarily hold property belonging to others. To estimate its property loss exposures, such a business has to consider not only its own property, but also the property held for others.

1-5. These answers address property loss exposures questions:

a. Insurance practitioners divide personal property into several categories: buildings, personal property contained in buildings, money and securities, vehicles and watercraft, and property in transit. Josh and Jill have a building which is their house that is exposed to loss. Their personal property contained in their home is exposed to loss. They likely also have some money and securities in the house or elsewhere that is subject to loss. Their two vehicles are subject to loss. Josh and Jill's property in transit exposure may not be as significant as the other property types but could include, for example, a set of golf clubs in the trunk of one of their vehicles while being transported to and from a golf course.

b. The building or house can be damaged or destroyed by perils such as fire, windstorm, hail, flooding, and theft. The other property types can be damaged by those perils as well. However, money and securities are particularly susceptible to loss by theft. Cash is difficult to trace because it can be readily spent. In contrast, other types of property must be sold for cash before the thief can make a profit. Money and securities are also lightweight, easily concealed, and easy to transport. Josh and Jill's vehicles and the property in transit contained in them are also exposed to the peril of collision.

c. Each type of Josh and Jill's property, if damaged or destroyed, could incur a reduction in value. If their property is damaged, the cost to repair or restore it is often the amount of reduction in value. Their property may have different values, depending on the method by which the value is determined. The most common valuation measures used in insurance policies are replacement cost and actual cash value (ACV).

Educational Objective 2

2-1. The legal system in the U.S. derives essentially from the Constitution, which is the source of constitutional law; legislative bodies, which are the sources of statutory law; and court decisions, which are the sources of common law.

2-2. These are the four elements that must be proven:

- The defendant owed a legal duty of care to the plaintiff.
- The defendant breached the duty of care owed to the plaintiff.
- The defendant's negligent act was the proximate cause of the plaintiff's injury or damage.
- The plaintiff suffered actual injury or damage.

2-3. Vicarious liability often arises in business situations from the relationship between employer and employee. An employee performing work-related activities is generally acting on behalf of the employer. Therefore, the employer can be vicariously liable for the actions of the employee.

2-4. Strict liability (absolute liability) is the legal liability arising from inherently dangerous activities or dangerously defective products that result in injury or harm to another, regardless of how much care was used in the activity.

2-5. One reason for such legislation is to ensure adequate compensation for injuries without lengthy disputes over who is at fault.

2-6. Gary would likely not succeed because a person must sustain actual harm for a liability loss to result in a valid claim.

2-7. Yes, liability for the intentional tort of invasion of privacy can arise from the unauthorized release of confidential information. Unless Susan gave Renee her consent to release her confidential medical information to another party such as Tess, Renee may be held liable if she does so.

Educational Objective 3

3-1. A significant liability loss exposure for almost all persons and businesses comes from the ownership, maintenance, and use of automobiles. In the United States, auto accidents produce the greatest number of liability claims.

3-2. Businesses often include photographs of people using their products in their advertisements. If a local retailer cannot afford professional models, it might use pictures of people using its products or shopping in its store. Unless the retailer obtains proper permission, publishing the pictures could lead to a lawsuit alleging invasion of privacy.

3-3. Even in the unlikely event that all the possible lawsuits against a defendant are ultimately found groundless, defendants and their liability insurers will probably incur substantial defense costs.

3-4. Anyone who owns or occupies real property has a premises liability loss exposure. Ted was operating a pet shop, which is the premises where the injury occurred. However, businesses must be concerned not only about the condition of their premises but also about their business operations. Whatever activity the business performs has the potential to cause harm to someone else. In this case, Ted's business operations, selling pets, resulted in an injury to a customer. So a liability claim may arise from a premises or a business operations activity.

Educational Objective 4

4-1. Over a short time period, an entire group may leave because of common dissatisfaction (such as poor management), may follow a manager to a new organization, or may be lost because of a catastrophic event.

4-2. Involuntary employee separations generally are not considered personnel losses because the organization has determined that it is better off without the employees. If, for example, a layoff is the result of a change in the organization's goals—meaning that the laid-off employees are no longer needed for the organization to operate efficiently—their departure will have a minimal effect on the organization's success. Employees are typically fired for cause (that is, for not performing their jobs effectively or behaving in an unacceptable manner).

4-3. While death and voluntary resignation often occur suddenly, retirement is usually planned. With plenty of notice, an organization can usually prepare for the retirement of even key personnel by locating and training replacements. However, as with resignation or death, when a key person decides to retire suddenly, the losses can be severe.

4-4. These answers address questions regarding the personnel case study.

a. Abe is a valuable asset of the agency because he adds value to the organization through his physical and mental labor. Abe is also a key employee because he is the owner and manager of the agency. He is responsible for making decisions essential to the agency, as well as managing and motivating others. In an organization, such as the agency, in which the owner is a key person, that person's activities, health, and managerial competence all influence the organization's value. A sole proprietorship, such as the agency, can literally cease to exist as a legal entity when its owner dies or retires. The business relationships Abe has developed with the insurers he represents and the customers he insures are also in jeopardy.

b. Abe's stroke is the cause of loss to his health. By causing a permanent disability, even if it is only partial, the cause of loss will continue until Abe can find and train a successor. Abe's sudden retirement due to the stroke may result in losses similar to the losses death or voluntary resignation would have brought.

c. Some of the financial consequences of Abe's permanent and partial disability include these:
   - Loss of the value Abe contributed to the agency. (In this case, it may be severe, with the agency's value lowered at least for the short term.)
   - Replacement costs (recruitment, interviewing, and training of a successor).
   - Losses to the agency's value caused by negative publicity (insurers and insureds may decide to terminate their relationship with the agency).
   - Losses caused by low morale of the remaining agency employees, which could result in reduced productivity and increased illness.

Educational Objective 5

5-1. The asset exposed to loss in a net income loss exposure is the future stream of net income of the individual or organization, which includes revenues minus expenses and income taxes in a given time period. If income taxes are considered to be part of an organization's expenses, a net income loss is a reduction in revenue, an increase in expenses, or a combination of the two.

5-2. A direct loss is a loss that occurs immediately as the result of a particular cause of loss, such as the reduction in the value of a building that has been damaged by fire. An indirect loss is a loss that results from, but is not directly caused by, a particular cause of loss. An example of an indirect loss would be the reduction in revenue that an organization suffers as a result of fire damage to one of its buildings.

5-3. To determine the severity of a net income loss, it is sometimes necessary to project what revenue and expenses would have been had no loss occurred. Once a loss occurs, the difference between the projected net income and the actual net income earned after the occurrence is the net income loss.

5-4. There are potential net income loss exposures for the restaurant that may result from a property loss, a liability loss, and a personnel loss.

- Property loss—A fire occurring in the kitchen of the restaurant would be a direct property loss. It would also result in a net income loss as the business could not operate without a kitchen and would have to close until it was repaired. David would not earn income from the restaurant while it was closed, which is an indirect net income loss.
- Liability loss—If a poorly maintained chair broke and dropped a customer on the floor, a resulting legal claim would be a direct liability loss. The loss of business that could occur once it became publicly known the reason the chair broke was poor maintenance would be an indirect net income loss.
- Personnel loss—The resignation of David's top chef to work for a competitor would be a personnel loss. The damage to the restaurant's reputation and loss of business would be an indirect net income loss. Another net income loss could occur if David gets in a bidding war to hire a top chef away from another competitor.

Educational Objective 6

6-1. Pure risk entails a chance of loss or no loss, but no chance of gain. Conversely, a speculative risk presents the possibility of loss, no loss, or gain.

6-2. For a loss to be fortuitous, the insured cannot have control over whether or when a loss will occur.

6-3. The three components required for a loss exposure to be definite are time, cause, and location. The insurer must be able to determine the event (or series of events) that led to the loss, when the loss occurred, and where the loss occurred.

6-4. An ideally insurable loss exposure must be one of a large number of similar exposure units because a loss exposure that is one of a large number of similar exposure units allows an insurer to spread the risk of loss over its entire pool of similar insureds and thereby maintain manageable premium levels.

6-5. The distinguishing characteristic of an independent loss exposure is that a loss suffered by one insured does not affect any other insured or group of insureds.

6-6. Loss exposures involving only small losses and loss exposures involving a high probability of loss are generally considered uninsurable because they are not economically feasible to insure. The expense of providing the insurance probably exceeds the amount of potential losses.

Direct Your Learning

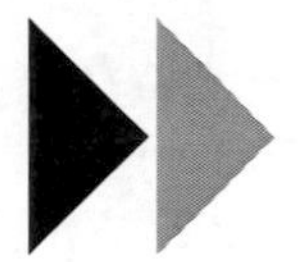

9

Insurance Policies

Educational Objectives

After learning the content of this assignment, you should be able to:

1. Explain the four elements of any valid contract.
2. Describe the distinguishing characteristics of insurance policies.
3. Explain how insurance policies can be structured using each of these alternatives:
    - Preprinted and manuscript forms
    - Self-contained and modular policies
    - Endorsements and other related documents
4. Given a specific policy provision, classify it into one of the following categories:
    - Declarations
    - Definitions
    - Insuring agreements
    - Conditions
    - Exclusions
    - Miscellaneous provisions
5. Explain how property policy provisions typically address each of the following:
    - Covered property
    - Covered locations
    - Covered causes of loss
    - Excluded causes of loss
    - Covered financial consequences

9

Educational Objectives, continued

- Covered parties
- Amounts of recovery

6. Explain how liability policy provisions typically address each of the following:
   - Covered activities
   - Covered types of injury or damage
   - Excluded loss exposures
   - Covered costs
   - Covered time period
   - Covered parties
   - Amounts of recovery

Outline

- **Elements of a Contract**
  - A. Agreement (Offer and Acceptance)
  - B. Capacity to Contract
  - C. Consideration
  - D. Legal Purpose
- **Distinguishing Characteristics of Insurance Policies**
  - A. Contract of Indemnity
  - B. Contract of Utmost Good Faith
  - C. Contract Involving Fortuitous Events and the Exchange of Unequal Amounts
  - D. Contract of Adhesion
  - E. Conditional Contract
  - F. Nontransferable Contract
- **Insurance Policy Structure**
  - A. Preprinted and Manuscript Forms
  - B. Self-Contained and Modular Policies
  - C. Endorsements and Other Related Documents
- **Policy Provisions**
  - A. Declarations
  - B. Definitions
  - C. Insuring Agreements
  - D. Conditions
  - E. Exclusions
  - F. Miscellaneous Provisions
- **Property Policy Provisions**
  - A. Covered Property
  - B. Covered Locations
  - C. Covered Causes of Loss
  - D. Excluded Causes of Loss
  - E. Covered Financial Consequences
  - F. Covered Parties
  - G. Amounts of Recovery
- **Liability Policy Provisions**
  - A. Covered Activities
  - B. Covered Types of Injury or Damage
    1. Bodily Injury
    2. Property Damage
    3. Personal and Advertising Injury
  - C. Excluded Loss Exposures
  - D. Covered Costs
    1. Damages
    2. Defense Costs
    3. Supplementary Payments
    4. Medical Payments
  - E. Covered Time Period
  - F. Covered Parties
  - G. Amounts of Recovery
    1. Policy Limits
    2. Defense Cost Provisions
    3. "Other Insurance" Provisions

If you find your attention drifting, take a short break to regain your focus.

For each assignment, you should define or describe each of the Key Words and Phrases and answer each of the Review and Application Questions.

Educational Objective 1

Explain the four elements of any valid contract.

Key Words and Phrases

Valid contract

Consideration

Review Questions

1-1. Describe when the process of achieving mutual assent in insurance generally begins.

1-2. Describe what could occur if an insurer mistakenly writes an insurance policy in a state where that insurer is not licensed.

1-3. In an insurance contract, describe the insurer's consideration.

Application Questions

1-4. Despite being a minor, Ralph completes an auto insurance application and sends it to an underwriter of an insurer. The underwriter accepts his application. Later when the insurer tries to collect the premium it earned by providing coverage to Ralph, he claims he does not owe it because the contract is not enforceable. Is Ralph correct? Explain.

1-5. Edgar was behind on his car payments and drove his car into a lake. He contacted the police and his auto insurance claims representative to inform them his car was stolen. The car was later recovered and the evidence indicated Edgar caused the damage to his vehicle. How does Edgar's action affect the insurance contract's legal purpose?

Educational Objective 2

Describe the distinguishing characteristics of insurance policies.

Key Words and Phrases

Principle of indemnity

Valued policy

Concealment

Misrepresentation

Material fact

Conditional contract

Review Questions

2-1. List the six distinct characteristics of an insurance policy.

2-2. Explain how a contract of indemnity does not necessarily pay the full amount necessary to restore an insured who has suffered a covered loss to the same financial position.

2-3. Why is insurance considered a contract of utmost good faith?

2-4. What is the distinction between concealment and misrepresentation?

2-5. Insurance buyers agree to pay a premium, and insurers agree to pay claims. Why does this contract involve an exchange of unequal amounts?

Application Question

2-6. An insured who has recently been involved in a minor auto accident states, "I have been driving for years and never had an auto accident. Now I finally have a chance to get back those thousands of dollars of premiums I have paid, so I am going to take the insurer for everything I can get." Explain why this person has a misconception concerning how insurance policies are designed to work.

Educational Objective 3

Explain how insurance policies can be structured using each of these alternatives:

- **Preprinted and manuscript forms**
- **Self-contained and modular policies**
- **Endorsements and other related documents**

Key Words and Phrases

Preprinted form

Manuscript form

Self-contained policy

Modular policy

Coverage part

Declarations page (declarations, or dec.)

Endorsement

Review Questions

3-1. Explain how preprinted policy forms and manuscript policy forms differ.

3-2. Describe the information typically contained in an insurance application and explain how that information is used by an insurer.

3-3. Explain how coverage is determined in a policy in which an endorsement conflicts with the original policy provisions.

Application Question

3-4. The Boom Company manufactures sparklers and fireworks used for community Fourth of July celebrations. It recently expanded operations and purchased an additional warehouse for inventory storage. Explain what type of form would likely be used by the insurer to cover all of Boom's coverage needs.

Educational Objective 4

Given a specific policy provision, classify it into one of the following categories:

- **Declarations**
- **Definitions**
- **Insuring agreements**
- **Conditions**
- **Exclusions**
- **Miscellaneous provisions**

Key Words and Phrases

Policy provision

Scheduled coverage

Insuring agreement

Condition

Exclusion

Moral hazard

Morale hazard (attitudinal hazard)

Review Questions

4-1. List six common categories of policy provisions found in insurance policies.

4-2. Describe the purpose of a policy insuring agreement.

4-3. Identify the obligations of these parties as stated in the conditions of an insurance policy:

a. Insurer

b. Insured

4-4. List the purposes of exclusions in an insurance policy.

4-5. Identify loss exposures typically excluded from a policy because they are considered uninsurable.

Application Question

4-6. Jane is in an auto accident while driving her insured car. Her son, John, a passenger, is injured. Jane is wondering whether John is an insured under the medical payments coverage of her auto policy. What section of the policy would clarify the term "insured" and help determine whether John is considered an insured under the policy?

Educational Objective 5

Explain how property policy provisions typically address each of the following:

- **Covered property**
- **Covered locations**
- **Covered causes of loss**
- **Excluded causes of loss**
- **Covered financial consequences**
- **Covered parties**
- **Amounts of recovery**

Key Words and Phrases

Floater

Named peril

Special form, or open perils policy

Collision coverage

Other than collision (OTC) coverage

Specified causes of loss coverage

Direct loss

Time element loss (indirect loss)

Net income

Extra expenses

Additional living expense (ALE)

Named insured

Loss payee

Deductible

Insurance-to-value provision

Coinsurance

Review Questions

5-1. Explain why exclusions and limitations are not the same thing.

5-2. Explain why a property insurance policy for covering personal property that moves from one place to another is often called a floater.

5-3. Explain why some perils that affect many people at the same time are generally considered to be uninsurable.

5-4. Explain why a business incurs extra expenses after experiencing a direct property loss.

5-5. Describe the purposes of a policy limit.

5-6. Explain why property insurance policies usually contain a deductible provision.

Application Questions

5-7. Peter owns an older home with a plumbing system that, over the years, has become prone to developing leaks. He is on a tight budget and needs to save money wherever possible, including in the amount of insurance premium he pays. He is trying to decide which policy form (basic, broad, or special) he should buy to insure his house. Which policy form would probably best fit Peter's needs? Explain.

5-8. Mary owns a duplex. She lives in one unit and rents out the other. She has explained to her agent that she needs the rental income from the other unit every month in order to pay the mortgage. If the rental unit was uninhabitable because of a fire, for example, she would lose her home. What assurance can her agent provide her about this risk when discussing the coverage provided in a homeowners policy?

Educational Objective 6

Explain how liability policy provisions typically address each of the following:

- **Covered activities**
- **Covered types of injury or damage**
- **Excluded loss exposures**
- **Covered costs**
- **Covered time period**
- **Covered parties**
- **Amounts of recovery**

Key Words and Phrases

Liability insurance

Bodily injury

Property damage

Personal injury

Release

Supplementary payments

Prejudgment interest

Postjudgment interest

Medical payments coverage

Occurrence- based coverage

Claims-made coverage form

Retroactive date

Each person limit

Each occurrence limit

Aggregate limit

Split limits

Single limit

Review Questions

6-1. Describe the two approaches used by liability insurance policies to define covered activities.

6-2. Describe what advertising injury, as covered by most commercial general liability (CGL) policies, typically includes.

6-3. Explain how pollution exclusions help keep premiums reasonable.

6-4. Explain why some states do not permit insurers to pay punitive damages on behalf of their insureds.

6-5. Explain how a liability policy with a single limit applies to a loss involving property damage and bodily injury to multiple individuals.

Application Questions

6-6. According to both CGL and homeowners policies, property damage includes both direct losses and time element (or indirect) losses sustained by the claimant. If a delicatessen has to close for twenty days because of water damage caused by a leaking pipe from the business next door, what are the restaurant's direct and time element (or indirect) losses?

6-7. Larry recently bought a small plane for personal use. He damaged another party's parked plane when he accidently collided with it. Larry reported the claim to his homeowner's insurer who told him there was no coverage. Explain why the homeowners policy does not cover this loss.

6-8. Fran was injured in two unrelated accidents. She was injured the first time when she hit her head in an auto accident, and the second time when she slipped and fell in her kitchen. She has both personal auto and homeowners insurance with the same insurer. She files a claim for medical payments for both injuries. Explain how Fran's personal auto and homeowners insurance will or will not cover each medical payment claim.

Answers to Assignment 9 Questions

NOTE: These answers are provided to give students a basic understanding of acceptable types of responses. They often are not the only valid answers and are not intended to provide an exhaustive response to the questions.

Educational Objective 1

1-1. In insurance, the process of achieving mutual assent generally begins when someone who wants to purchase insurance completes an insurance application—an offer to buy insurance. The details on the application describe the exposures to be insured and indicate the coverage the applicant requests.

1-2. If an insurer mistakenly writes an insurance policy in a state where that insurer is not licensed, the insured might later argue that the contract is not valid and demand the return of the premium. This demand would be based on the fact that the insurer did not have the legal capacity to make the agreement.

1-3. In an insurance contract, the insurer's consideration is its promise to pay a claim in the future if a covered loss occurs. If no loss occurs, the insurer is still fulfilling its promise to provide financial protection even though it does not pay a claim.

1-4. Being a minor can remove capacity of an individual to contract causing the contract to be unenforceable. However, minors are sometimes considered competent to purchase auto insurance, especially when auto insurance qualifies as a necessity. State laws vary in regard to issues involving minors. If Ralph applied for the insurance in a state that recognizes auto insurance as a necessity, he may owe the premium being billed by the insurer.

1-5. No insurance contract will remain valid if the wrongful conduct of the insured causes the operation of the contract to violate public policy. So, by intentionally driving his car into the lake, Edgar rendered his auto insurance policy unenforceable and would preclude his recovery under his policy for the damage he intentionally caused.

Educational Objective 2

2-1. An insurance policy is a contract of indemnity, a contract of the utmost good faith, a contract involving fortuitous events and the exchange of unequal amounts, a contract of adhesion, a conditional contract, and a nontransferable contract.

2-2. Most policies contain a policy limit that specifies the maximum amount the insurer will pay for a single claim. Many policies also contain limitations and other provisions that could reduce the amount of recovery. For example, a homeowners policy is not designed to cover large amounts of cash. Therefore, most homeowners policies contain a special limit, such as $200, for any covered loss to money owned by the insured. In that instance, if a covered fire destroys $1,000 in cash belonging to the insured, the insurer will pay only $200 for the money that was destroyed.

2-3. Insurance is considered a contract of utmost good faith because insurance involves a promise that requires complete honesty and disclosure of all relevant facts from both parties. Both parties to an insurance contract—the insurer and the insured—are expected to be ethical in their dealings with each other.

2-4. The distinction between concealment and misrepresentation is that concealment is an intentional failure to disclose a material fact (omission) but a misrepresentation is a false statement of a material fact (falsehood).

2-5. The insurance contract involves an exchange of unequal amounts because, often, there are few or no losses and the premium paid by the insured for a particular policy is more than the amount paid by the insurer to, or on behalf of, the insured. If a large loss occurs, however, the insurer's claim payment might be much more than the premium paid by the insured. It is the possibility that the insurer's obligation might be much greater than the insured's that makes the insurance transaction a fair trade.

2-6. This insured does not understand that an auto policy is designed to work as a contract involving the exchange of unequal amounts. The premium paid by the insured for a particular policy can be, and often is, more than the amount paid by the insurer to, or on behalf of, the insured for a covered loss. The contract is also designed to work as a conditional contract. The insurer must perform only under certain conditions, such as when a covered loss occurs during the policy period. A covered loss might not occur during a particular policy period, but that fact does not mean the insurance policy for that period has been worthless. In buying an insurance policy, the insured acquires a valuable promise—the promise of the insurer to make payments if a covered loss occurs. The promise exists, even if the insurer's performance is not required during the policy period.

Educational Objective 3

3-1. Preprinted policy forms are standardized contracts developed for different types of insurance that do not require negotiating new contractual terms for each policy purchased. Manuscript policy forms are customized contracts developed for a specific insured or group of insureds who share unique coverage needs.

3-2. An insurance application typically contains information about the insured and the loss exposures presented to the insurer.

3-3. If the policy and the endorsement contain conflicting terms, the endorsement takes precedence.

3-4. The insurer would likely use a manuscript policy for Boom's insurance contract because the company's coverage needs are specialized due to the explosive nature of its manufactured items. Typically, the insurer would not have standard forms available to cover this exposure and would have to customize the policy for the Boom's specific coverage needs.

Educational Objective 4

4-1. These are six categories of policy provisions found in insurance policies:

- Declarations
- Definitions
- Insuring agreements
- Conditions
- Exclusions
- Miscellaneous provisions

4-2. The purpose of a policy insuring agreement is to state in broad terms the insurer's promises to the insured.

4-3. These are the obligations of the parties as stated in the conditions of an insurance policy:

a. Obligations of the insurer as stated in the conditions of an insurance policy are to pay covered losses, to defend the insured from lawsuits, and to provide other services to the insured.

b. Obligations of the insured that are commonly stated in the conditions of an insurance policy are to pay premiums; to report losses promptly; to provide appropriate documentation for losses; to cooperate with the insurer, as in legal proceedings; and to refrain from jeopardizing an insurer's rights to recover from responsible third parties (subrogate).

4-4. Exclusions in an insurance policy can serve one or more purposes:

- Eliminate coverage for uninsurable loss exposures
- Assist in managing moral hazards
- Assist in managing morale hazards
- Reduce the likelihood of coverage duplications
- Eliminate coverages that the typical insured does not need
- Eliminate coverages requiring special treatment
- Assist in keeping premiums reasonable

4-5. Loss exposures typically excluded from a policy because they are considered uninsurable include nonaccidental events such as war, earthquake, or flood.

4-6. The definitions section helps clarify terms that have specific meaning within Jane's auto policy. The definition of the term "insured" in that section may help verify whether John is covered under the policy.

Educational Objective 5

5-1. While exclusions eliminate all coverage for excluded property or causes of loss, limitations place a specific dollar limit on specific property that is covered.

5-2. A property insurance policy for covering personal property that moves from one place to another is often called a floater because it provides coverage that floats, or moves, with the property as it changes location.

5-3. Some perils that affect many people at the same time are generally considered to be uninsurable because the resulting losses would be so widespread that the funds of the entire insurance business might be inadequate to pay all of the claims. For this reason, almost all property insurance policies exclude coverage for losses from catastrophes such as war and nuclear hazard.

5-4. The reason a business incurs extra expenses after experiencing a direct property loss is to continue its operations, which may also reduce the business income loss.

5-5. A policy limit has several purposes. It tells the insured the maximum amount of money that can be recovered from the insurer after a loss. By comparing the policy limit to the value that may be lost, the insured can determine whether the amount of insurance is adequate. The policy limit is also important because it allows insurers to keep track of their overall obligations in any one geographic area and because the premium charged is directly related to the policy limit for most property insurance coverages.

5-6. Property insurance policies usually contain a deductible provision, which serves several functions. Deductibles encourage the insured to try to prevent losses because the insured will bear a part of any loss. Shifting the cost of small claims to the insured also enables the insurer to reduce premiums. Handling claims for small amounts often costs more than the dollar amount of the claim. Thus, deductibles enable people to purchase coverage for serious losses at a reasonable price without unnecessarily involving the insurer in small losses.

5-7. The basic form covers the fewest perils of the three forms and therefore has the lowest premium. However, the basic form does not cover sudden and accidental leakage of water from a plumbing system. Therefore, the basic form is probably not the form best suited for Peter. The broad form covers more perils than the basic form but fewer than the special form. The broad form's premium is likely higher than the basic form's, yet lower than the special form's. The broad form does cover the peril of sudden and accidental leakage of water from a plumbing system, so it is probably the best choice for Peter.

5-8. Her agent could explain that homeowners policies provide coverage for lost income. When a covered cause of loss, such as a fire, damages the part of a residence that Mary rents or holds for rental to others, "fair rental value" coverage in the homeowners policy indemnifies her for the loss of rental income until the rented portion of the residence has been restored to livable condition.

Educational Objective 6

6-1. Liability insurance policies use two approaches to defining covered activities. Certain policies state the specific activity or source of liability covered, such as an auto insurance liability policy stating that it applies to claims that result from covered auto accidents. General liability insurance, in contrast, covers all activities or sources of liability that are not specifically excluded.

6-2. Advertising injury, which is covered by most CGL policies, typically includes libel and slander; publication of material that constitutes an invasion of privacy; misappropriation of advertising ideas or business style; and infringement of copyright, trade dress, or slogan.

6-3. Commercial liability policies generally exclude all but limited exposures from pollution. Businesses with more serious pollution liability exposures must purchase specialty policies to cover those exposures. If broad pollution coverage were provided under all liability policies, the coverage would not be affordable.

6-4. Some states do not permit insurers to pay punitive damages because the punishment is viewed as less effective if the responsible party does not personally pay the required damages.

6-5. The most an insurer will pay is the combined single limit for all property damage and bodily injury to which the insurance applies; regardless of the number of persons injured. A single limit applies to any combination of bodily injury and property damage liability claims arising from the same occurrence. For example, a $300,000 single limit covers a bodily injury loss up to $300,000, a property damage liability loss up to $300,000, or any combination of bodily injury and property damage arising from a single occurrence up to $300,000.

6-6. The direct losses include the cost of repairing the water damage to the delicatessen's property, which may also include replacing some inventory. The time element (or indirect) losses include the loss of income for the twenty days that the delicatessen had to be closed for repairs.

6-7. No insurance policy can reasonably cover all loss exposures. Liability insurance policies generally follow the broad guideline to eliminate duplicate coverage provided by policies specifically designed to address particular exposures such as aircraft liability. Larry should have bought a separate policy that specifically covers aircraft liability.

6-8. Personal auto policy medical payments coverage will cover her as an insured for her head injury, up to a specified limit. However, her homeowners policy's medical payments coverage will not cover her slip-and-fall injury because she is an insured or regular resident of her household.

Exam Information

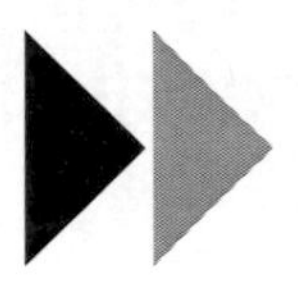

About Institutes Exams

Exam questions are based on the Educational Objectives stated in the course guide and textbook. The exam is designed to measure whether you have met those Educational Objectives. The exam does not necessarily test every Educational Objective. It tests over a balanced sample of Educational Objectives.

How to Prepare for Institutes Exams

What can you do to prepare for an Institutes exam? Students who pass Institutes exams do the following:

- Use the assigned study materials. Focus your study on the Educational Objectives presented at the beginning of each course guide assignment. Thoroughly read the textbook and any other assigned materials, and then complete the course guide exercises. Choose a study method that best suits your needs; for example, participate in a traditional class, online class, or informal study group; or study on your own. Use The Institutes' SMART Study Aids (if available) for practice and review. If this course has an associated SMART Online Practice Exams product, you will find an access code on the inside back cover of this course guide. This access code allows you to print a full practice exam and to take additional online practice exams that will simulate an actual credentialing exam.

- Become familiar with the types of test questions asked on the exam. The practice exam in this course guide or in the SMART Online Practice Exams product will help you understand the different types of questions you will encounter on the exam.

- Maximize your test-taking time. Successful students use the sample exam in the course guide or in the SMART Online Practice Exams product to practice pacing themselves. Learning how to manage your time during the exam ensures that you will complete all of the test questions in the time allotted.

Types of Exam Questions

The exam for this course consists of objective questions of several types.

The Correct-Answer Type

In this type of question, the question stem is followed by four responses, one of which is absolutely correct. Select the *correct* answer.

Which one of the following persons evaluates requests for insurance to determine which applicants are accepted and which are rejected?

a. The premium auditor

b. The loss control representative

c. The underwriter

d. The risk manager

The Best-Answer Type

In this type of question, the question stem is followed by four responses, only one of which is best, given the statement made or facts provided in the stem. Select the *best* answer.

Several people within an insurer might be involved in determining whether an applicant for insurance is accepted. Which one of the following positions is primarily responsible for determining whether an applicant for insurance is accepted?

a. The loss control representative

b. The customer service representative

c. The underwriter

d. The premium auditor

▶▶

The Incomplete-Statement or Sentence-Completion Type

In this type of question, the last part of the question stem consists of a portion of a statement rather than a direct question. Select the phrase that *correctly* or *best* completes the sentence.

Residual market plans designed for individuals who are unable to obtain insurance on their personal property in the voluntary market are called

a. VIN plans.

b. Self-insured retention plans.

c. Premium discount plans.

d. FAIR plans.

"All of the Above" Type

In this type of question, only one of the first three answers could be correct, or all three might be correct, in which case the best answer would be "All of the above." Read all the answers and select the *best* answer.

When a large commercial insured's policy is up for renewal, who is likely to provide input to the renewal decision process?

a. The underwriter

b. The loss control representative

c. The producer

d. All of the above

"All of the following, EXCEPT:" Type

In this type of question, responses include three correct answers and one answer that is incorrect or is clearly the least correct. Select the *incorrect* or *least correct* answer.

All of the following adjust insurance claims, EXCEPT:

a. Insurer claim representatives

b. Premium auditors

c. Producers

d. Independent adjusters